D0171694

THEY WILL KNOW US BY OUR LOVE

Service Ideas for Small Groups

www.group.com

Group resources actually work!

This Group resource helps you focus on **"The 1 Thing®"**— a life-changing relationship with Jesus Christ. "The 1 Thing" approach incorporates our **R.E.A.L.** approach to ministry. It reinforces a growing friendship with Jesus, encourages long-term learning, and results in life transformation, because it's:

Relational
Learner-to-learner interaction enhances learning and builds Christian friendships.

Experiential
What learners experience through discussion and action sticks with them up to 9 times longer than what they simply hear or read.

Applicable
The aim of Christian education is to equip learners to be both hearers and doers of God's Word.

Learner-based
Learners understand and retain more when the learning process takes into consideration how they learn best.

They Will Know Us by Our Love
Service Ideas for Small Groups
Copyright © 2007 Group Publishing, Inc.

All rights reserved. No part of this book may be reproduced in any manner whatsoever without prior written permission from the publisher, except where noted in the text and in the case of brief quotations embodied in critical articles and reviews. For information, e-mail Permissions at inforights@group.com or write Permissions, Group Publishing, Inc., Product Support Services Dept., P.O. Box 481, Loveland, CO 80539.

Visit our Web site: **www.group.com**

Credits
Contributors: Cheri R. Gillard, Jan Kershner, Joy-Elizabeth F. Lawrence, Summer Rivers Salomonsen, Chris Sigfrids, Carl Simmons, S. Renee Tripp, Amber Van Schooneveld, and Heather Werle
Editors: Heather Werle and Roxanne Wieman
Creative Development Editor: Matt Lockhart
Chief Creative Officer: Joani Schultz
Assistant Editor: Dena Twinem
Book Designer: Andrea Boven Nelson of Boven Design Studio
Cover Art Director: Jean Bruns
Cover Designer: Jay Smith of Juicebox Designs
Illustrator: Alan Flinn
Production Manager: DeAnne Lear

Unless otherwise indicated, all Scripture quotations are taken from the *Holy Bible,* New Living Translation, copyright © 1996, 2004. Used by permission of Tyndale House Publishers, Inc., Wheaton, Illinois 60189. All rights reserved.

Library of Congress Cataloging-in-Publication Data
They will know us by our love : service ideas for small groups.
   p. cm.
Includes indexes.
ISBN 978-0-7644-3434-1 (pbk. : alk. paper)
1. Church work. 2. Theology, Practical. 3. Service (Theology) 4. Small groups. I. Group Publishing.
BV4400.T44 2007
253'.7--dc22
                          2006033426

10 9 8 7 6 5 4 3 2 1   16 15 14 13 12 11 10 09 08 07
Printed in the United States of America.

Contents

Section Five:

Serving Those with Specific Needs

They Will Know Us by Our Love

"So now I am giving you a new commandment: Love each other. Just as I have loved you, you should love each other. Your love for one another will prove to the world that you are my disciples" (John 13:34-35).

Jesus called us—his followers—to love one another as he loved us: selflessly, actively, sacrificially.

Jesus said that the world would know his disciples by our *love*—not by our perfectly lived lives, or our deep understanding of doctrine, or even by our unfailing devotion to him. He didn't say those things were bad, he didn't say those things weren't important parts of faith. They're just not how people recognize his followers. No, it's *love* that sets apart Christ-followers from everyone else.

Love.

But love isn't just a feeling. It's an action. It's demonstrable. It's noticeable.

And as Jesus modeled in John 13, one of the best ways to demonstrate love—to make love noticeable—is through service.

"And since I, your Lord and Teacher, have washed your feet, you ought to wash each other's feet. I have given you an example to follow. Do as I have done to you" (John 13:14-15).

101 Service Ideas for Small Groups

Jesus called us to love one another and to extend that love beyond the church and into the community. Your small group is the perfect place to answer that calling. And this book can help you do it.

They Will Know Us by Our Love contains within it 101 creative ideas for serving those around you—your **community**, your **church**, one another in your **small group**, your **friends and family**, and **people with specific needs** who need help.

Each idea will give you everything you need to get your small group started. You'll get **practical ideas** to help you plan the idea, **helpful hints** to make the service project go smoothly, **Scripture** that connects with the activity, a **prayer** to help you dedicate the service project to God, and **reflection questions** so you and your small group can debrief the project once you've completed it.

You'll also find a **Scripture index** at the back of the book if you'd like to choose ideas based on biblical passages you're studying. Or you can use the additional indexes to locate ideas based on their **duration, type of service activity,** or even **what time of year** you want to do a project.

At the end of the book, we've given you a **checklist** you can complete after you've finished a service idea. This tool will help you document how the project went, when you did it, who participated, and any comments you have for next time.

Icons

Throughout the book, you'll notice several icons. These icons are meant to help you identify certain types of service projects. We've divided the book into five sections: **serving your community, serving your church, serving your small group, serving your friends and family,** and **serving those with specific needs**. Additionally, within each of these sections you'll find activities differentiated by the following icons:

Duration

 One-Time activities: These activities are meant to be done on a Saturday, an evening, or once a year. They generally last one day or a few hours.

 Short-Term activities: These projects are meant to be done over a short period of time—a week or a month maybe.

 Ongoing activities: These service ideas will take a greater commitment from your small group. They last an indefinite amount of time, and your small group may only want to take on one or two of these.

Type of Service Activity

 Getting-to-Know-People activities: These service projects will help you get to know the people you're serving. They include intentional conversation time, opportunities for fellowship, and service through relationship.

Behind-the-Scenes activities: When your small group does one of these, you'll be sure to get your hands dirty! These activities will have your small group serving people by *doing things* for them: cleaning, building, dishing out food.

 Honoring-People activities: Veterans, Sunday school teachers, seniors...these ideas will help your small group serve people as you honor them.

 Supporting-People activities: These activities will have your small group serving people as you support existing institutions or people who are already serving. From animal shelters, to church youth groups, to fund-raising marathons, your small group will serve those who are serving.

 Giving-to-People activities: Giving is an act of service. Your small group can give refurbished furniture, old cell phones, care baskets, food...the ideas are endless, and there are bunches of them in here!

You'll also find great service ideas for:

Fall

Winter

Spring

Summer

Loving Service

Change the face of your small group. Inspire your members to show Jesus' love through service. Empower them to live lives of sacrificial love...of selfless service.

> "What good is it, dear brothers and sisters, if you say you have faith but don't show it by your actions? Can that kind of faith save anyone? Suppose you see a brother or sister who has no food or clothing, and you say, 'Good-bye and have a good day; stay warm and eat well'—but then you don't give that person any food or clothing. What good does that do? So you see, faith by itself isn't enough. Unless it produces good deeds, it is dead and useless" (James 2:14-17).

Serving Your COMMUNITY

Serving your community isn't always easy. In fact, sometimes it seems wiser to band together *against* the community—it's us against them. They don't like us because we're Christians, after all. But the truth is, love can break down those barriers. Service can change people's hearts.

Bring Jesus' love to your streets...to the neighbors down the block, to the people at the grocery store, to the kids in the park, to those rougher neighborhoods you don't normally visit.

Serve them...with love.

"We live in such a way that no one will stumble because of us, and no one will find fault with our ministry. In everything we do, we show that we are true ministers of God. We patiently endure troubles and hardships and calamities of every kind. We have been beaten, been put in prison, faced angry mobs, worked to exhaustion, endured sleepless nights, and gone without food. We prove ourselves by our purity, our understanding, our patience, our kindness, by the Holy Spirit within us, and by our sincere love."

—2 Corinthians 6:3-6

Light Up Your Neighborhood

"Jesus spoke to the people once more and said, 'I am the light of the world. If you follow me, you won't have to walk in darkness, because you will have the light that leads to life'" (John 8:12).

Do you ever find yourself waving to that semi-familiar-looking family down the street...but you've never actually taken the time to introduce yourself?

Use this service idea to make your community safer and brighter—and get to know the people you live near but may not often interact with.

Your small group should split up into pairs or groups of three for this activity. Have each group canvass an area of town where at least one member resides. Meet at that member's home, each person armed with several boxes of fresh light bulbs, empty plastic bags or boxes to hold disposals, and a pair of lightweight gloves to use while handling hot bulbs.

Then walk your neighborhood streets, approaching each resident one by one and offering to replace burnt-out light bulbs on their porch or driveway. At each door, present the friendly explanation of a chance to introduce yourselves, as well as the benefits of brighter streets (such as increased safety) in your community. If a home's porch lights aren't visibly extinguished, stop to offer your services anyway—don't miss the opportunity to say hello to a neighbor...besides, perhaps their *back* porch light is burnt out!

Dear Jesus, Walk with us as we walk our neighborhoods. Help us to light up our streets as you've promised to light up our lives. We pray that our neighbors would know that true safety and comfort come from knowing you. In your name, amen.

Helpful Hints

- Make sure to carry light bulbs of varying wattages to cover different models of lighting fixtures.
- A great time to perform this service is at the beginning of spring after the long, dark winter nights have left many outside lights extinguished.

Reflect

- How did your neighbors initially respond to you approaching their homes?
- What transformations did you witness in your neighbors' attitudes as they realized you were there to offer a "no strings attached" service?
- What is one specific way you were able to verbally or physically share Jesus' light through these interactions with your neighbors?

Work Recycling Program

This program will benefit your workplace, wider community, and generations to come!

Discuss the state of recycling in your various workplaces. Some places of employment may have recycling containers for everything: office paper, newspaper, beverage containers, and metals. Others may just have one or two. Make a list of how many and what type of recycling containers each person will need for his or her workplace. Then assign one person to purchase the containers, and ask everyone to chip in and share the cost.

> "But with eager hope, the creation looks forward to the day when it will join God's children in glorious freedom from death and decay. For we know that all creation has been groaning as in the pains of childbirth right up to the present time" (Romans 8:20b-22).

Get permission from your office manager and decide on a location to put the containers. Suggest putting paper containers near the copy room as well as a small container by each desk. Beverage containers go well in halls or break rooms. Let the office manager know that you'll take responsibility for the project.

Deliver the containers to the workplaces. Have the individual from each workplace send a mass e-mail informing fellow employees of the new program and encouraging them to recycle.

Empty the recycling containers at least once a week in order to keep office places clean and clutter-free! Group members who aren't working with recycling programs in their offices can assist others in taking the recycling to a center or including it with their home recycling.

DEAR CREATOR GOD, Thank you for this beautiful Earth. Give us the grace, patience, and hope to be good stewards of your creation. May our workplace recycling programs glorify your name and bring hope to others. IN JESUS' NAME, AMEN.

Reflect

- How has this activity caused you to think about your role as a steward?
- If anyone asked you why you were doing this, what was your response?
- What sort of response did people have toward the new program?

Helpful Hints

- If you don't know the recycling policies (or locations) in your city, look online for information. Usually it helps to search your city name and "recycling."
- Start your program with a bang: Put brownies or other goodies by each recycling bin with a note that encourages people to begin recycling.

3

Neighborhood Share-a-Thon

"And God will generously provide all you need. Then you will always have everything you need and plenty left over to share with others" (2 Corinthians 9:8).

Here's a great way for your neighbors to spend more time together and save money while they're at it!

Organize a convenient way for neighbors to share seldom-used resources by establishing a list of who is willing to share what particular possessions (such as lawn equipment, baby supplies, power tools, books, and movies).

Ask each group member to e-mail or mail an invitation to all his or her neighbors. You can use the sample invitation we've provided (on page 13) as a springboard for writing your invitations.

Once each person's neighbors have responded with their lists, he or she can compile a master list of who owns what, phone numbers, and any other information. Then group members can distribute the list to their neighbors and encourage them to begin sharing!

DEAR LORD OF ALL, *You have made everything, and everything is yours. Give us generous hearts to share, and bless our neighborhoods with the graciousness to share among themselves. May this project grow our relationships with our neighbors and help out those who have less than us.* IN JESUS' NAME, AMEN.

Reflect

- Initially, how did people feel about sharing with their neighbors?
- How did this project affect the neighbors' relationships to one another?
- How did you see God working in the lives of your neighbors?

Helpful Hints

- Use an online community site to create a group and list the objects you have to share. This will make it easier to instantly distribute updates to your community.
- For more personal contact, hand-deliver the invitations.
- Set up some ground rules for returning items promptly, and what to do if something is broken while someone is borrowing it. Include this information on the master list so that everyone has it!

Dear Neighbor,

Have you noticed that simplicity is all the rage lately? Well, since we're all geographical neighbors, I'm setting up a sharing program for our neighborhood. We'll probably be sharing _____, but let me know if you're interesting in sharing other types of things such as: (list other options you're thinking about here). You don't have to participate, but if you do, you may be able to find that one thing you need only once a year...and let someone use that other thing you keep in the basement for 364 days out of the year. Interested? E-mail me at _____.

Thanks!

Your name,

Your phone number,

e-mail address,

and street address

School Smart

"Work with enthusiasm, as though you were working for the Lord rather than for people. Remember that the Lord will reward each one of us for the good we do, whether we are slaves or free" (Ephesians 6:7-8).

Everyone knows how little attention public schools receive, yet most of us count on them to academically prepare the next generation.

As a group, draft a letter to the principal of a public school in your community. In the letter, explain that your group would like to be of service for whatever need the school may have at this moment. Make sure to leave out the "God" aspect in this letter (or your service may be refused); just present yourselves as residents of the community who want to help. Call a week later to make sure the letter was received. If that school doesn't bite, send the letter to another, and another. You'll be surprised at the needs within schools—there's plenty to do for folks who just want to help. Be ready for anything: running scoreboards at a game, picking up trash, helping teachers move rooms...

Dear God, We ask that you would bless this letter as we write it and when we send it. We ask that you would allow us to fill the needs of those educators who so desperately need to be served. Please bless our efforts and give us the opportunity to serve this school. In Jesus' name, amen.

Reflect

- What types of needs did you expect to find in schools? Were your expectations accurate? Why or why not?
- What were the reactions of teachers, principals, and students as you served the school?
- In what other ways could you serve those who faithfully teach our kids?

Helpful Hints

- Remember—this is a public school and it is maintained with a strict separation of church and state. Utilizing actions instead of words may feel different, but God's love will shine through your service even in the absence of words.
- Be ready and joyful for *any* task. You will be a great blessing to an educator or student!

Run, Small Group, Run!

Look on community Web sites or contact local police departments, schools, and other organizations to find out about local races. Many areas have 5Ks, 10Ks, and other runs/walks to raise money for various groups. Pick one that is for a cause close to your heart and that you honestly believe in. As a group, train and run in the event together.

> "I press on to reach the end of the race and receive the heavenly prize for which God, through Christ Jesus, is calling us" (Philippians 3:14).

Instead of simply signing up and paying the entrance fee, be creative in raising funds and try to get family, friends, and neighbors involved as well. You could raise support for each mile you run in your training, work at a local sporting event (and have them pay your organization of choice instead of you), or organize a carwash.

If you're not a runner and can't walk the event, volunteer to serve. All along the route there will be people handing out cups of water and sports drinks. Other volunteers work at the registration area and the finish line.

Dear God, Thank you for the ability to enjoy your creation and be active. Please be with those who are in this race. Protect them from injury. Teach us to run, serve, and walk for you—in everything we do. Bless the organization in ways that draw people closer to you. Thank you for the privilege it is to help meet the needs of others. In Jesus' name, amen.

Reflect

- What was the most fun about the experience?
- How can you serve the organization after the event?
- How can you continue relationships with those you met at the event?

Helpful Hints

- Be realistic with your physical self and the others in your group. Training *with* friends is much more fun than doing it alone.
- Have fun at the event! Wear matching T-shirts, invite your friends to watch, and don't stress about your time.
- If you are talking to the organization about ways to serve, ask about the most dreaded volunteer roles and volunteer for them!
- At the event, strike up conversations and get to know those around you. Use it as an opportunity to build relationships that might lead to sharing God's love on a long-term basis.

6

Love Your Enemies

"You have heard the law that says, 'Love your neighbor' and hate your enemy. But I say, love your enemies! Pray for those who persecute you! In that way, you will be acting as true children of your Father in heaven" (Matthew 5:43-45a).

Serving people you are comfortable with is one thing, serving the poor and outcast another... but serving your enemies—that's the toughest act of love.

During your meeting time, discuss perceived enemies—who do the people in your small group find hard to love? Some group members may name personal enemies; others may say they have a hard time loving people in prison, people who have different political views, or people of different religions.

After discussing these enemies, decide who you want to serve. You may decide to break up into groups and serve different people, depending on the size of your group and the variety of hard-to-love people you want to serve.

Now start talking specifics. Where is the best place to serve? How do you go about serving your enemy? How long will this last? How can you serve your enemy out of love and not duty?

Here are a few suggestions to get you started:

- Write a kind note or e-mail to the person or group.
- Set aside time each day to pray for your enemy.
- Follow Jesus' example and invite them to share a meal with you.

DEAR JESUS, Help us to love the way you loved and serve the way you served. Teach us to love even those we consider enemies. IN JESUS' NAME, AMEN.

Reflect

- Was it easy to choose an enemy? Why or why not?
- What kinds of conversations or interactions did you have with the person or group you chose to serve?
- After serving, was your attitude toward your enemy different? Why or why not?

Helpful Hints

- Be careful about whom you choose to serve—you want to be challenged, but you don't want to put yourself in a position where you could be in danger.
- Pray and ask God to put a specific enemy on your heart who he wants you to reach out to in love.

Post-Game Pickup

Almost everyone enjoys some sort of sport: football, basketball, baseball, soccer—you name it! So go to a sporting event together, and then serve together by picking up trash after the end of the game.

In your small group, a few weeks before the event, decide which game you want to attend. You can attend a professional game in a major city, a local high-school game, or a nonprofessional competition in your area.

> "You must have the same attitude that Christ Jesus had. Though he was God, he did not think of equality with God as something to cling to. Instead, he gave up his divine privileges; he took the humble position of a slave and was born as a human being" (Philippians 2:5-7).

Designate a meeting spot before the game, and then try to have everyone sit in the same location at the game—that way you can have fun cheering on your team together!

After the game ends, wait until most people have left the stadium before you begin cleaning. Get started in a large area where people have already left their seats. Stay together as a team to clean or break up into small groups by sections—it's up to you.

Don't announce yourselves to the crowd, but don't be shy either. Smile, work quickly, and answer questions as to why you're serving.

DEAR GOD, *Give us joyful hearts as we serve and pick up trash. We pray for those who attend this game today—that they may know your love.* IN JESUS' NAME, AMEN.

Reflect

- What was on your mind before you started cleaning?
- What kinds of comments or looks did you get from people? How did the people who were responsible for cleaning up after the game respond to you?
- How can we similarly serve people in our daily lives?

Helpful Hints

- If you attend a professional game, be sure people buy tickets in advance.
- Safety first: Wear rubber gloves when handling trash.
- Go as a team—wear matching T-shirts.
- Remember to bring trash bags.
- Leave full bags of trash at the end of each aisle.
- Figure out how many people you have and how much time you want to serve. Be realistic about how much you can clean.

Nothing but Positive

"Do you have the gift of speaking? Then speak as though God himself were speaking through you. Do you have the gift of helping others? Do it with all the strength and energy that God supplies. Then everything you do will bring glory to God through Jesus Christ. All glory and power to him forever and ever! Amen" (1 Peter 4:11).

This service project will take endurance; love; and a whole lot of smiles, applause, and "atta-boys" or "atta-girls."

Your mission is simple: Choose a school game, play, or event to go to with your small group. It could be a high-school basketball game, a 5th-grade musical, or an adult softball game.

Sit as a group, the bigger the better, and do this: Cheer, hoot, holler, clap your hands, start the "wave," buy people around you popcorn... you get the idea! Basically, in everything you do, be an encouragement to those around you—especially those who are competing or performing.

OH LORD, Please help us to be an encouragement in everything we do. Fill us with love and joy so that others will see and know you are in us. IN JESUS' NAME, AMEN.

Helpful Hints

- If you go to a game, split up and cheer for opposite teams.
- You'll probably draw attention to yourselves—that's OK—just be careful not to be obnoxious or distracting. You want others around you to think "Who are these people and why are they being so kind and encouraging?" not "I wish these people would be quiet and go away."
- After the game or the event, go and tell the participants that they did a great job. Be specific about what you thought they did well, such as "That song you sang in the third scene sounded amazing" or "That was a great hit you had in the fifth inning—you've got a real talent for the game."

Reflect

- What reaction did you get from the crowd? from participants?
- Did you catch yourself saying or thinking negative things or did you stick to the mission to be encouraging at all times and in all ways? Why?

Adopt a Family Farm

Did you know that thousands of small family farms are rapidly disappearing from the countryside due to economic pressures?

"People who work hard sleep well" (Ecclesiastes 5:12a).

There are several ways your small group can help. First, find a farm! Go to www.localharvest.org/csa/, go to your state's department of agriculture page, or search the Internet for "farm directory" in your region. A CSA farm (Community Supported Agriculture) might work well, as many of these farms have volunteer work programs already set up. (CSAs are farms that allow the public to buy shares in the farm. This secures funds for the farms and a weekly produce supply for the shareholders.) Next, decide how big of a commitment your small group can make. Perhaps you want to volunteer to work together once a month, once a week, or have small-group members rotate working once a week.

Contact farms you think might be a good fit. Ask the farms what help they need most. There are a number of tasks volunteers can do with little training. Maybe they need people to box and organize produce for the market or help man the farmers-market booth, corn mazes, or seasonal festivals. There might also be low-level field work your group can do.

Be creative with the help you offer. Perhaps the best way to help a family working hard all day would be to prepare them a meal once a week. Or maybe they need help advertising their CSA farm. Above all, find ways to refresh and encourage a family working hard to maintain a dying and noble way of life!

DEAR GOD, You've blessed each of us with so much that we want to bless others in turn. Thank you for this hardworking and persevering family. Help us to be a refreshment and encouragement to them. IN JESUS' NAME, AMEN.

Reflect

- What was your most memorable experience in serving this farm?
- What did you learn about hard work?
- In what ways did this experience inspire you to persevere and work hard in your own life?

Helpful Hints

- Farms will need your help most in the summer, so it would be best to contact potential farms in the spring to set up something.
- Make sure to communicate clearly that you want to volunteer at the farm with no strings attached and no ulterior motives.
- If you volunteer to help a CSA farm, while you're at it, encourage members to purchase a farm membership. They'll get great produce all season, and the farm will have more guaranteed income!

19

10

Recycling Day

"The Lord God placed the man in the Garden of Eden to tend and watch over it" (Genesis 2:15).

Not only will this project be a great help to your community, but you will be acting as a responsible steward of what the Lord has entrusted to humanity.

Plan a recycling event. Provide an opportunity for people to bring their recyclable items—such as aluminum cans, newspapers, glass, and cardboard—as well as those things that are difficult to dispose of, such as computer components and old appliances. Involve computer recycling companies and appliance restoration organizations so that these difficult-to-recycle items can be collected and disposed of in an appropriate manner.

Research what type of items can be recycled in your area. Arrange with appropriate facilities for their involvement with your event, including pickup of items, any payment for items, and possible presence during your event.

Advertise several weeks in advance so people can begin to collect items with your event in mind. Hang fliers at local grocery stores, announce with radio spots, arrange newspaper releases, and spread the information by word-of-mouth. A week before the event, increase awareness by distributing door-to-door notices. Involve other local churches by asking them to hang your fliers and announce the event to their congregations.

Choose a place to hold your event, such as a parking lot, and mark designated drop-off areas. Prepare collection bins, as well as signs and instructions to direct people to the appropriate areas. Make certain everyone directing the acceptance of the items is clear on what can and can't be received.

DEAR GOD OF CREATION, You made this Earth and all that is in it and declared it good. Help us to tend and watch over it well. Help us to show others we value your creation as we work together to be good stewards. IN JESUS' NAME, AMEN.

Helpful Hints

- Mark lanes with cones to facilitate easy drive-through drop-off points.
- Provide information to participants about the problems of landfills and of ways to continue their recycling efforts in the future.
- Donate any money earned to recycling programs and awareness.

Reflect

- How did this project alter your perspective of caring for God's creation?
- How did individuals respond to your event?

Facelift for an Eyesore

Is there a location in your community with a reputation for being unattractive and a constant eyesore? Perhaps there's a crumbling wall or a broken fence with trash caught in the weeds overtaking it, or a wall always covered

"At last the wall was completed to half its height around the entire city, for the people had worked with enthusiasm" (Nehemiah 4:6).

with graffiti. Choose such a location, obtain permission from the owner, and plan a workday to give the area a facelift.

Prior to the workday, collect outdoor paint and brushes, flower bulbs or plants native to your area that need little to no care, trash bags, hardware, and any other supplies you'll need for your particular project.

Make any necessary repairs, weed the area, and clean up the trash. Plant flowers or flower bulbs—depending on the time of year. Curtail graffiti by painting a mural, flowers, or geometric designs on surfaces commonly used for graffiti. Tap the neighborhood's artistic skills by inviting local kids and adults alike to help plan and implement the project.

Plan a schedule for watering and maintaining the plants as needed until they are established. Include people from the neighborhood, if possible, so that they feel ownership and pride in the project.

At the end of the workday, break out beverages and snacks and invite others to celebrate the accomplishment with you. Have a party and take some "marvel time" to enjoy how the facelift looks!

DEAR GOD, Help us to work with enthusiasm, with all our hearts. Help us to work hard for others for your sake and, in doing so, bless those around us. IN JESUS' NAME, AMEN.

Reflect

- How did outsiders respond to your project? to your invitation to participate with you?
- What were your feelings as you labored for others—perhaps some who didn't care what you did or had other priorities?
- How might this kind of project further God's kingdom?

Helpful Hints

- To include others, put up a large sign with a "crier" on the workday, inviting anyone interested in helping to join your project.
- Determine what design you want to paint. Put one-inch graph lines on the design. Then with chalk or charcoal, put an enlarged graph on the wall and transfer the design prior to painting.

12

Join In!

"For God is the one who provides seed for the farmer and then bread to eat. In the same way, he will provide and increase your resources and then produce a great harvest of generosity in you. Yes, you will be enriched in every way so that you can always be generous. And when we take your gifts to those who need them, they will thank God" (2 Corinthians 9:10-11).

Use your small group's time to show appreciation and support for others already serving or supporting those in your community. Identify an all-day charity event that will be held in your community in the next month or so—for instance, a local Relay for Life for cancer, a CROP walk, or a benefit concert or auction. Make arrangements with the event's organizers to set up a booth at the event, either at the location where it's being held or along the route that participants are traveling through your town. Set up one or two tables, and put out a banner or poster to invite participants to take a break at your table(s).

Hand out bottles of water to participants when they stop by. Also have a selection of fresh fruits and other healthy snacks available to support and refresh those participating in the event or attending in support. Find out in advance how many are expected to attend or participate so you have enough supplies on hand to serve everyone who stops by. Some of these events go all night, so think about the degree of commitment you can make as a group, then stick to it.

Be sure to take time to speak with those who visit your booth as well, and encourage them in the good work they're doing. It will give everyone involved an extra spiritual and emotional boost even as you're serving their physical needs.

Dear Lord, Help us to honor and serve those who help others. As we do this, move in the hearts of those we serve to give them a deeper appreciation of all you have done for us and how you desire us to serve you as well. In Jesus' name, amen.

Reflect

- How did it feel to encourage people who were taking their own time to help others?
- How did this activity inspire you to do other good works for God?

Helpful Hints

- Local stores are often willing to contribute food and supplies for a good cause—which could enable your small group to do a *big* job. Once you've established what you'd like to give away, approach store managers about partnering with you.
- Set up a tent to help protect participants from the elements so those you're serving get even more needed relief (and you can last longer, too!).

Town Festival

Many communities hold annual (sometimes even seasonal) town festivals, and many of them are open to civic groups of all kinds. Use the day as an opportunity for your small group to serve and get to know others in your town.

Make arrangements with the festival coordinators (probably a few weeks in advance) to set up a table or booth for that day—they're often free to civic groups, especially when nothing is being sold. Then decide on how you want to serve those who stop by to say hello.

"You are the light of the world—like a city on a hilltop that cannot be hidden. No one lights a lamp and then puts it under a basket. Instead, a lamp is placed on a stand, where it gives light to everyone in the house. In the same way, let your good deeds shine out for all to see, so that everyone will praise your heavenly Father" (Matthew 5:14-16).

Be as elaborate or simple in your planning as your group has the energy and manpower for. You could have some inexpensive but meaningful giveaways available, such as baked goods and coffee, or upgrade your food offerings to a lunch of sodas and sub sandwiches.

You might give away balloons or small gifts to kids who are walking around. You could even hire a clown to give out the balloons, and take instant-print photos of the kids posing with the clown. This would require a little more financial investment from your group, but it would free up your group members to spend more time talking to visitors.

LORD, You have placed us in this community for your purpose. Help us to serve those you have placed us among. And as we see others and serve them the way you would, help them to see your Spirit present in us. IN JESUS' NAME, AMEN.

Reflect

- What insights did you gain into your community as you served?
- How do you think the way you see your town differs from the way God sees it?
- What's another way you might be able to serve your community in the future, based on what you learned?

Helpful Hints

- If you can rent or borrow a helium tank, your balloons will be even more attractive to kids. Have lots of extras available for when kids inevitably lose them into the air.

14

Furniture Fix-Up

"The godly love to give!" (Proverbs 21:26b).

If you've ever passed an auction or garage sale offering lots of furniture, you've probably noticed a crowd. Furniture is an often-sought-after commodity, perhaps because its function is such a basic necessity. So use the necessity of furniture to offer others a more important necessity—the love of God.

Scour your attic, basement, and garage. Surely there's a table you haven't used in years or a chair just begging for repair. Ask neighbors, friends, and even your congregation to contribute. Go to local thrift shops, garage sales, and auctions. Who knows what treasures you may find? Then get to work!

Set up a well-ventilated work area and purchase safety wear (gloves, face masks, and goggles). A book on the basics of furniture repair is a good idea, too.

Unless you have a practiced woodworker in your group, start with small projects. Sometimes all a piece of older furniture really needs is a good cleaning to be functional again, and anyone can handle that!

Once you have several pieces of furniture ready for new homes, decide how you'll distribute your goods. You could donate to a local charity, church, or have your own give-it-away garage sale. The recipients of your hard work will remember the love you shared each time they use that piece of furniture.

DEAR LORD, Thank you for the opportunity to serve others. Help us think of those who don't have the basics in life, and to make giving a way of life. IN JESUS' NAME, AMEN.

Reflect

- How did working with your hands differ from other ways you've served in the past?
- Were there any pieces of furniture that you would have liked to keep for yourself? What was it like to give them away?
- What did you learn about your small-group members by working together on this project?

Helpful Hints

- Dispose of the used stripping agent in a sealed container.
- Be careful not to sand too heavily on veneered wood—you may sand right through the veneer.

Cell Phone Recycling

You know the drill. It's time to renew your cell phone agreement, so you do a little research. It seems that everyone has a deal, and that deal includes a new phone—smaller, more sophisticated, and filled with more cool functions than the one you have.

"Do not withhold good from those who deserve it when it's in your power to help them" (Proverbs 3:27).

So what do you do with your old phone? Throw it in a drawer "just in case I might need it some day"? Toss it in the trash? According to the U.S. Environmental Protection Agency, there are up to 130 million cell phones retired every year.

But used cell phones can benefit your community in a big way. Did you know that even without a service agreement, wireless carriers are required to transmit 911 calls?

All you need is a charged-up cell phone in good operating condition. Incoming calls can't be received, nor can any other outgoing calls be made. But the ability to call for help could make a life-or-death difference to someone who might otherwise have no way to contact emergency personnel.

Consider collecting used cell phones and donating them to shelters for battered women, the elderly, or the homeless. Alternatively, you could collect and donate the used phones to various groups who pay for the phones and then either donate or dispose of them themselves. Check out the EPA Web site and type in "eCycling" for ideas and referral.

DEAR LORD, Thank you for the opportunity to serve you. Thank you for always being there for us in every circumstance. IN JESUS' NAME, AMEN.

Reflect

- What kinds of emergencies do you think this service project may help with in the future?
- What was the most gratifying part of this project for you?

Helpful Hints

- By collecting and donating used cell phones, not only will your group be providing a much-needed service in your community, but will also be keeping harmful chemicals out of your local landfill. Cell phones contain in their circuitry, batteries, and liquid crystal displays such toxins as arsenic, beryllium, cadmium, copper, and lead. Their plastic casings have also been treated with brominated flame retardants.

Serving the Servers

Jesus said: "When you put on a luncheon or a banquet...don't invite your friends, brothers, relatives, and rich neighbors. For they will invite you back, and that will be your only reward. Instead, invite the poor, the crippled, the lame, and the blind. Then at the resurrection of the righteous, God will reward you for inviting those who could not repay you" (Luke 14:12-14).

Based on Luke 14:7-14, together plan a dinner for six to eight people, and invite people who work in service professions as special guests. Invite restaurant servers, day-care or nursing-home workers, retail sales clerks, or people who clean homes or hotels. Set a formal table—no plastic utensils or paper plates for this one. Treat your guests as royalty, just as you would expect to be treated if you were eating at a fancy restaurant. Be careful not to be condescending. If they want to know why they are there, explain that you are working on a lesson to learn a greater appreciation for people whose jobs call for serving others. Talk to them about their jobs and how those they serve treat them. Try as much as possible to put yourselves in their shoes and learn from them. See if this exercise changes your attitude the next time you are impatient with a busy sales clerk or your waiter brings the wrong meal to your table.

DEAR JESUS, You set the ultimate example of a servant's heart. You served in a way that no one could ever pay you back. Thank you for showing us how to serve as you did. Open our eyes to more places to serve, and please help us have the courage to take advantage of these opportunities. IN YOUR NAME, AMEN.

Reflect

- How did you feel inviting somewhat anonymous people who serve you to a personal setting where you were serving them?
- What did you learn from your guests?
- How can you serve those who serve on a more regular basis?

Helpful Hints

- Invite people you already have established relationships with because it will not seem awkward for you or the invitees. If you stop at the same coffee shop every morning, see if the baristas would like to come together.
- Pick a theme, and have each person in your small group be responsible for bringing one part of the meal to take the burden off the host or hostess.

One Man's Treasure...

Challenge yourselves to each find 50 things in your home that you don't need. Give away those items to a Christian charity before the group meets again. Make a list of all the things you gave away. When you next meet, have everyone share his or her list. Challenge and encourage each other to be content and to have an appropriate attitude toward possessions. You may even want to challenge each other to give away another 50 things.

You may want to have everyone in your group gather all the giveaway items together and take them as a group to a Christian charity.

"Don't store up treasures here on earth, where moths eat them and rust destroys them, and where thieves break in and steal. Store your treasures in heaven, where moths and rust cannot destroy, and thieves do not break in and steal. Wherever your treasure is, there the desires of your heart will also be" (Matthew 6:19-21).

DEAR GOD, You have blessed us in ways that are beyond our imagination, but we often fail to even recognize the ways that you have provided for us. Please open our eyes to all that we have and put in us a spirit of thanksgiving.

Please help us become more aware of the ways that we can use the tangible blessings in our lives to meet the tangible needs in the lives of others. Help us learn to hold loosely all that you have given us. IN JESUS' NAME, AMEN.

Reflect

- What insights did you have as you considered what to give away and as you actually did give it away?
- What did you learn about what you truly *need* versus the things you *want*?

Helpful Hints

- Try not to pick stuff that more appropriately belongs in the trash. Yes, they might be 50 things that you are done using or don't need, but they should be items that are usable to the people receiving these gifts.
- Look through your clothes. Except for special-occasion items, look for things that you haven't worn in a year. Chances are if you haven't worn it in the past 12 months, you won't miss it if it's gone.
- Challenge yourself to donate a few things that you *will* miss greatly but don't truly *need*. For instance, if you have two pairs of very similar snow boots and are donating things to a shelter in a colder climate, share the blessing and give someone the gift of warm feet this winter.

Help Carry the Burden

"Share each other's burdens, and in this way obey the law of Christ. If you think you are too important to help someone, you are only fooling yourself. You are not that important" (Galatians 6:2-3).

You've been there before: an armful of groceries, pouring rain, and you can't find your keys to open your car door…

As a group, practice demonstrating your love for others by choosing a few hours on a busy Saturday morning to help people carry their groceries to their cars and return the carts to the store. (Be sure to get permission from the store manager ahead of time.)

As you help people, be friendly, cheerful, and engage in conversations if people so desire. And if people ask what you're doing…well, tell them! Let them know you are serving in the name of love…God's love for them!

Afterward, meet together over coffee to talk about how the morning went.

DEAR GOD, You see the needs of people before they even recognize them on their own! Lord, please give us your eyes to see where we can serve others while going about daily tasks. IN JESUS' NAME, AMEN.

Reflect

• How was your gesture of love received by others?

• How could you serve in similar ways on a more regular basis?

• Share about one person you encountered who you will not soon forget.

Helpful Hints

• Target the elderly and mothers who are juggling young children.

• Be careful not to "take away" the jobs of those employed at the store, and be respectful of those roles.

• Have the men in your group pair up with women, and if not, encourage men to recognize that some women alone in parking lots may feel as if they are being followed or stalked as part of a criminal act. If someone refuses the help and is suspicious, explain why you are serving in this way, and if they still seem leery, allow for the space and back off right away.

A Bag Party

During the fall season, find a public space in your town that could really use some raking and general cleaning. Have a bag party and work together to clean up the area.

Encourage each group member to bring a lawn and leaf bag and some gloves. Work together to beautify all the public space in the area you have chosen. Be ready to explain to neighbors or passersby why you've chosen to spend your time together in this way.

"Then God blessed them and said, 'Be fruitful and multiply. Fill the earth and govern it. Reign over the fish in the sea, the birds in the sky, and all the animals that scurry along the ground' " (Genesis 1:28).

DEAR GOD, Thank you for providing beautiful areas in our neighborhood that we can so freely enjoy. Thank you for bringing community to the area through these spaces. Use them for your glory. Foster relationships that bring people into a relationship with you. Open our eyes to see this place as a gift from you and an opportunity to meet new people and share our faith. IN JESUS' NAME, AMEN.

Reflect

- Why did you pick this particular location?
- What was it like to talk to people using the area as you worked?
- What was most memorable about the experience?

Helpful Hints

- If it's public property, check with your local government to get permission.
- Pick a place that is more often neglected in your community, such as a park *not* in the nicest part of town.
- If people in your small group have children, ask the adults to take turns watching them during the project day.

A Gesture of Love

"But you will receive power when the Holy Spirit comes upon you. And you will be my witnesses, telling people about me everywhere—in Jerusalem, through Judea, in Samaria, and to the ends of the earth" (Acts 1:8).

As a group, serve the people at an Islamic mosque. Contact the leaders of the mosque. Explain that as a gesture of goodwill and love, your group would like to serve them by doing their yardwork, cleaning their building, or preparing a meal for them.

As you gather together before the workday, pray and ask God to give you a spirit of love and acceptance. As you work throughout the day, be sure to work hard, work according to any specifications given to you by the leaders of the mosque, and be friendly as people come and go from the mosque. Engage people in conversations—but not with the express purpose of conversion. Serve with love...not with ulterior motives.

Afterward, consider inviting someone from the mosque to speak to your group about relations between Muslims and Christians. Make friends with those who visit your group, and show them the love of Christ.

DEAR GOD, We pray for the tensions between different religious groups in the world today. We ask for peace where there is conflict and for lives spared where there is violence. Use us in this small way to build a bridge between two communities of faith. Teach us to be sensitive and caring with your love so that we can share the gospel with all people of all faiths. IN JESUS' NAME, AMEN.

Reflect

- What did you learn from this different faith community?
- What are their basic beliefs?
- How can you more effectively bridge the gap between your church and other religions in your community—in a way that will spread God's love?

Helpful Hints

- Be respectful of the guidelines they might ask you to follow while being in their place of worship.
- Study the particular sect of the mosque ahead of time in order to have a better understanding of the specific culture.

Editorialize

Christians and non-Christians often use the editorial page of the local newspaper to bash each other. Have everyone gather copies of your local newspaper several days this week and look for such letters. Also look for letters, or for syndicated columns, that simply express an opinion that's counter to Christianity. Gather to write letters to the editor (or to the columnist) that lovingly express a Christian point of view. Be sure to be respectful in your tone and to express the love of Christ to the person. If possible, have individuals from your group contact these people personally, invite them to coffee, seek to understand their point of view, and make friends with them. By making a loving and personal connection, perhaps you can introduce them to the love of Jesus.

"Now who will want to harm you if you are eager to do good? But even if you suffer for doing what is right, God will reward you for it. So don't worry or be afraid of their threats. Instead, you must worship Christ as Lord of your life. And if someone asks about your Christian hope, always be ready to explain it. But do this in a gentle and respectful way. Keep your conscience clear. Then if people speak against you, they will be ashamed when they see what a good life you live because you belong to Christ. Remember, it is better to suffer for doing good, if that is what God wants, than to suffer for doing wrong!" (1 Peter 3:13-17).

DEAR GOD, *Thank you for the freedom in this country. We often take it for granted and forget to take advantage of the platform it provides for us to share our faith. Please help us wisely answer for the hope that we have in you in order to share your love with the people in our community. IN JESUS' NAME, AMEN.*

Reflect

- What issues do you think Jesus would address if he were writing a letter to your local newspaper?
- It's nearly impossible to learn everything about every topic. What is one area—or a few—that God has put on your heart, and how can you learn more about these to better discuss and offer a Christian perspective?
- What did you learn about the people who wrote the letter(s)?

Helpful Hints

- Be careful not to mention church names in your letters, unless the pastors, elders, board members, or other leadership is on board.
- Be concise yet thorough. Letters need to be short enough to fit in a small space, but they also need to cover all the necessary information.
- After writing the letters, ask someone to proofread them.
- Be loving. Avoid argumentative words and tone. Your point isn't to win the argument...your point is to win souls for God.

Prayer Walk

"I urge you, first of all, to pray for all people. Ask God to help them; intercede on their behalf, and give thanks for them. Pray this way for kings and all who are in authority so that we can live peaceful and quiet lives marked by godliness and dignity. This is good and pleases God our Savior, who wants everyone to be saved and to understand the truth" (1 Timothy 2:1-4).

Choose an area or neighborhood in your town in which you would like to see God work. Form pairs or trios, and have each pair or trio spend one afternoon or evening walking through that area or neighborhood, praying for the people who live or work there. If possible, schedule your prayer walks during daylight hours. Also take whatever safety precautions you feel are necessary.

As each pair or trio walks, have group members pay attention to their surroundings and to the people they see. If you're praying through a neighborhood, pray for the people who live in each home. Pray for those you see outdoors. Pray for situations that arise during your walk. For example, you might hear arguments or you might see children who need attention or supervision. Pray that God would be at work in the neighborhood and that the residents would desire to seek God and be drawn into relationships with him. Pray that Christians in the neighborhood would be strengthened in their faith and would be called to reach their neighbors with the gospel. Pray that churches in the neighborhood would be healthy and strong.

DEAR JESUS, Thank you for welcoming us into a friendship with you. Thank you for loving us so much that you want to hear from us. Thank you for the ability to pray. We confess that sometimes we forget the power of prayer. We attempt to control situations and forget to pray. Please use this as a reminder to always be praying for this community. IN YOUR NAME, AMEN.

Reflect

- What did you observe during this experience that you had never previously noticed while walking or driving through the neighborhood?
- What needs did you feel most concerned about? What does that teach you about the God-given passions in your heart?
- How can you follow through on some of the needs you observed?

Helpful Hints

- If it's the beginning of the school year, pray though a neighborhood that has a school and for the students who are about to begin class.
- If you run into people you know, ask how you can be praying for them.

Neighborhood Carwash

Choose the neighborhood of someone in your group, and agree to serve the people who live there by washing the residents' cars. Pick a day and time, and make simple fliers to pass out to the neighbors, letting them know that your group will be washing cars. Let them know the location and the time of the event. Make sure it's clear that this is a free neighborhood service with no strings attached.

"Give thanks to the Lord and proclaim his greatness. Let the whole world know what he has done. Sing to him; yes, sing his praises. Tell everyone about his wonderful deeds" (1 Chronicles 16:8-9).

On the day of the event, go door-to-door and let the neighbors know what you're doing. Invite them to bring their cars by for a free wash. Wash and dry each car thoroughly, but accept no donations. If anyone asks why you're doing the carwash, feel free to say something like, "Because of the good things God has done for us, we want to turn around and do good things for others."

DEAR JESUS, Thank you for modeling the perfect example of being a servant. Thank you for the blessing of friendship, cars, water, and community. Thank you for laughter. Please open up opportunities to share of your love as cars are being washed. IN YOUR NAME, AMEN.

Reflect

• How did it feel to offer a free service and then refuse any sort of payment?
• What was it like to explain that you were sharing God's blessing as the reason you washed cars?
• What is one friendship that you formed or deepened during this experience?

Helpful Hints

• Check with your local government to see if you can close off the street like you would do for a block party. This way, you'll have all the space you need to park cars...and you'll draw even more attention to the event!
• Invite other small groups or friends to help with this fun project.
• Have music playing to create a fun atmosphere. And if possible, have available information on your church, drinks, and snacks.

Welcome to the Neighborhood!

"Dear children, let's not merely say that we love each other; let us show the truth by our actions. Our actions will show that we belong to the truth, so we will be confident when we stand before God" (1 John 3:18-19).

Your church can subscribe to receive a mailing list of new residents in the area. Check your Yellow Pages for local marketing firms, and call around to see if they offer this. Similarly, in most areas, sale transactions of residences are recorded in the local newspaper. Use this information to monthly or quarterly send a "welcome to the neighborhood" packet that would be useful for people moving from outside the area, or those just moving from another local address. Many local businesses will give you discount coupons to include. Add a personal touch by recommending restaurants or shopping secrets for the area.

DEAR JESUS, Thank you for the gift of friendship—friendship with you and friendship with others. Please help us be open to forming relationships with new people. Show us where to reach out and who is craving companionship. Open the congregation to welcome new people into the church family. IN YOUR NAME, AMEN.

Helpful Hints

- Work with multiple churches in the area. The goal should be to build up the entire body of Christ and to help new residents find a church home that is a good fit. This might mean your church, and it might mean another Christian church down the street. Providing all the information at once will help people know the service times, a little about the various ministries, and what churches are available.
- Include a response card that new residents can fill out if they'd like more information. Follow up by visiting in pairs or as a family.
- Consider hand-writing the address and personal note in each packet so that it comes across as a sincere welcome instead of stale marketing.

Reflect

- What would be most helpful to you if you recently moved to the area?
- How did you feel the first time you went to your church? How can you make visitors feel even more welcome?

Ambush Lawn Service

Organize yard crews to ride in pickups or vans with mowers, rakes, lawn trimmers—anything they might need to manicure a yard. Visit the homes of people in your neighborhood who might not have the time or capabilities to keep up on yardwork, and send in the ambush yard team to the rescue! Ask permission first before you begin cleaning up their yards.

"A friend is always loyal, and a brother is born to help in time of need" (Proverbs 17:17).

Your ambush team could also plant shrubs and flowers to make things really beautiful. Be sure to ask the yard owners if they want these plantings, as some regular care will be involved after the ambush team is long gone. If the owners go for it, ask local nurseries for donations of materials or if they offer discounts to nonprofit/community groups.

Send your crew out in teams of three or four, and have them meet back for homemade ice cream when all their hard work is done!

DEAR GOD, Thank you for the ability to do physical work. Please give this group the strength to clean up lawns. Please make our attitude like yours. God, please form new friendships between the group and the residents. Use this to show them and us more of your glory and love. IN JESUS' NAME, AMEN.

Reflect

- How did the residents respond to your ambush?
- What did you learn about yourself and the others in your group through this experience?
- What was the most enjoyable part of the project? How can you use that particular skill or interest to serve others on a regular basis?

Helpful Hints

- Single parents, the elderly, and families where one or both parents travel often are good targets.
- If you're short on lawn tools, ask around at your church to borrow supplies.
- This is a particularly effective project in the fall if you live in an area with trees that lose their leaves.

Serving Your
CHURCH

Acts 4:32-35. There were no needy people among them. *None.*

It's the calling of the church—it's God's desire for the church that there be no needy among us. That we are so generous, so loving, so serving that there isn't a *single* person in the church who needs anything: physically, emotionally, relationally. There's probably not a church today that's there yet—it's a lofty goal, to be sure, but it's definitely a goal worth striving for.

"All the believers were united in heart and mind. And they felt that what they owned was not their own, so they shared everything they had. The apostles testified powerfully to the resurrection of the Lord Jesus and God's great blessing was upon them all. There were no needy people among them, because those who owned land or houses would sell them and bring the money to the apostles to give to those in need."

—Acts 4:32-35

Group Workday

"And you yourself must be an example to them by doing good works of every kind. Let everything you do reflect the integrity and seriousness of your teaching" (Titus 2:7).

Put your sacrificial love into practice by scheduling a group workday.

Get your church directory, and find people on the list who are unable to work on their own houses. Then call those people and schedule a day when you can come and work on their homes. Ask them what they most need done, and work hard to finish those projects. Be sure you do the projects well and to the people's specifications.

Alternatively, you could also check with your church office to see if there are projects that need to be done in and around the church. Plan to give up a morning or afternoon to work on those projects.

DEAR GOD, Thank you for the gift of work. Thank you for the opportunity to serve you by serving others. Please bless the physical labor we are going to do. Keep us safe, and protect our group from conflict. Help us to use this time not only to do physical labor but also to share your love with those we are serving. IN JESUS' NAME, AMEN.

Reflect

- When was a time that you benefited from receiving help from others?
- How can you serve people at your job?
- What would you do differently for our next group workday?

Helpful Hints

- Ask the person at your church who interacts most with the elderly for suggestions on who might need help.
- A family with a new baby would be very appreciative.
- Anyone who recently bought a house and is on a tight budget would love the help fixing up his or her place.
- Make sure that your group pays for all the supplies needed to do the work.
- Have each person in your group bring a friend to double the impact in half the time!

Sunday Morning Service

At your next small-group gathering, discuss ways that your group can volunteer to serve your church in a way that will require personal sacrifice. For example, volunteer to serve in the nursery even though you'll miss out on attending Sunday school. Or volunteer to fix the coffee and pick up the doughnuts one morning even though you'll have to get up an hour earlier. Or volunteer to shovel the walks at your church when it snows. Another idea is to volunteer to organize and pass out supplies for the children's classes. Consider serving in this sacrificial way on a regular basis.

"Don't be selfish; don't try to impress others. Be humble, thinking of others as better than yourselves. Don't look out only for your own interests, but take an interest in others, too. You must have the same attitude that Christ Jesus had" (Philippians 2:3-5).

DEAR GOD, *You sent your Son to show us the ultimate example of sacrificial service. The sacrifice you made cost you more than we could ever fathom. Teach us to sacrifice in ways that are costly. Teach us more about what it means that you died and made such a sacrifice.*

Bless the ways that we are serving and help them to impact lives beyond what we can imagine! IN JESUS' NAME, AMEN.

Reflect

- What is one way that you could sacrificially serve on a regular basis, perhaps weekly or monthly?
- What were some of the needs that you discovered when looking for ideas on how to serve?
- How can you get others on board with your sacrificial service ideas?
- What were the more and less enjoyable parts of this experience?

Helpful Hints

- Let your church know if it's something that they should announce or prepare for, such as coffee and doughnuts after the service.
- Recruit all necessary volunteers to make sure everything is taken care of and that the job is done completely.
- Plan to purchase all necessary supplies ahead of time.
- If you pick something that is a weekly commitment, make sure it is one you can keep for an entire year, season, or school year.

Undercover Pastoral Care

"Elders who do their work well should be respected and paid well, especially those who work hard at both preaching and teaching" (1 Timothy 5:17).

Organize a day of mission and espionage! When your church's pastor is at work, do some undercover service projects. Wash the pastor's car in the parking lot, and deliver home-baked cookies anonymously to the front office of the church. Make plans with the pastor's spouse or family to mow the lawn.

Put together a fun gift for your pastor and family as well. Include restaurant, movie, or store gift certificates; favorite candies and other goodies; a book or CD that you know your pastor will like; and anything else you can think of! Drop the package off at your pastor's house with an encouraging note.

Dear Jesus, Thank you for setting the ultimate example of how to serve. Thank you for giving our church this pastor. We ask that you give our pastor your vision for ministry—your vision for how to best serve you and others. Also, we ask for strength and courage for our pastor in carrying out that vision. In your name, amen.

Reflect

- How can you best serve those who serve?
- What is one way that you can serve those who serve at your church?
- Where do your gifts and passions best fit in serving the church?

Helpful Hints

- If available, ask the pastor's administrative assistant about the best ways to serve your pastor.
- Try to do something surprising—something that the pastor may not spend time or money on doing normally.

A Gift of Service

Discover people who have the gift of serving and are already quietly serving behind the scenes at your church. Plan a way to honor them with a special gift of service.

"Dear brothers and sisters, honor those who are your leaders in the Lord's work. They work hard among you and give you spiritual guidance" (1 Thessalonians 5:12).

You might rake their lawns or provide a special meal. You might provide before-church child care for those who work during the church service and come early to prepare. Or you might even offer to take over their responsibilities at the church for a week.

DEAR GOD, *Thank you for those who serve behind the scenes. They do this not to show off to others but rather to serve you. Teach us from their example.*

Use these gifts and honors to show how much their service is appreciated, and help us take note of things like this more in the future. IN JESUS' NAME, AMEN.

Reflect

- What did you learn about your church from this experience?
- How was your gift of service received?
- What is one way that you could serve behind the scenes in a particular ministry?

Helpful Hints

- Ask spouses and friends of those who serve for ideas to make it personal.
- If you are unsure of who is serving behind the scenes, that is a good sign that they are truly "behind the scenes." Ask ministry leaders for the names of people who help them most in the "little things."

An Opportunity to Serve

"And since I, your Lord and Teacher, have washed your feet, you ought to wash each other's feet. I have given you an example to follow. Do as I have done to you" (John 13:14-15).

A church is always in need of volunteers. Consider volunteering in various ministry roles for a quarter or longer at your church.

Before your session, have someone gather from your church leaders a list of serving roles that need to be filled in your church. At your meeting, explore what each of those roles entails, and offer opportunities for those in your group who have the gift of serving or who are interested in volunteering. Be sure the group doesn't lay guilt on those who don't respond to the opportunities. Not everyone has the gift of service, and some may be serving in many ways already.

DEAR JESUS, You sacrificed everything as an act of love. Thank you for serving us. Thank you for teaching us how to serve. Please forgive us when we ignore your call to serve. Help us take advantage of opportunities to serve you by serving others. IN YOUR NAME, AMEN.

Helpful Hints

- Check with your children's and youth directors; they often have need of new volunteers.
- If there is no official list of roles to be filled, ask church leaders to dream and dream big—what do they wish someone in the congregation would do?
- Be careful to take on only things that you can handle. If you are not able to make a weekly commitment to a particular ministry, pick a one-time event or a smaller service opportunity.
- Remember that the service God desires is one done in love (1 Corinthians 13:1-3). If you feel you're doing this service out of guilt or obligation, pray and ask God to change your perspective to one of love. You may also want to consider a different volunteering opportunity.

Reflect

- On a scale of 1 to 10, how would you rank this experience for yourself? Why?
- How did our activity affect the way you think about your own spiritual gifts?
- How might this activity change your involvement in ministry?
- Who in this group do you think has the gift of serving? Explain.

Bibliophiles

Adopt your church library!

Assess the resources offered in your library. Are they current? attractively arranged? accessible to a cross section of your congregation? If you find that your resources are lacking, sponsor a library renovation "shower" through which the congregation is encouraged to donate resources and materials for effective research and study.

You may want to suggest that your church promote its resources by putting book reviews in the weekly bulletin or newsletter. Educate your congregation by having each member of your group choose a book from the library and write a review.

DEAR GOD OF WISDOM, Thank you for the gift of wisdom and the privilege it is to learn. Thank you for these resources and the ability to study your Word. Please use these resources for your glory. Bring people to them who have a desire to learn. Encourage our congregation to dig deeper in Scripture to learn more about you. Build up leaders and teachers to help teach others, as well. IN JESUS' NAME, AMEN.

> "Tune your ears to wisdom, and concentrate on understanding. Cry out for insight, and ask for understanding" (Proverbs 2:2-3).

Reflect

- What books interest you the most?
- What book sticks out as one that would be most challenging?
- What questions have you had about Christianity and God in the past? Where did you turn for answers?

Helpful Hints

- You might try contacting a seminary for books that they are no longer using but would still be valuable resources.
- Connect with a Christian college, and see if a professor would be interested in using these book reviews as part of a class.
- Keep the reviews short and simple enough that they are accessible, but also make sure to include enough information that a person can decide whether or not he or she wants to read the actual book.
- Create an electronic database for easy access.

Assistant to the Teacher

"But Jesus said, 'Let the children come to me. Don't stop them! For the Kingdom of Heaven belongs to those who are like these children' " (Matthew 19:14).

Ask everyone in your group to consider offering themselves as teacher assistants in the children's and youth departments for a week, month, or quarter. Be prepared to assist in any way the teacher asks, from interacting with a specific child, to helping with classroom decoration, to substitute teaching for a session.

DEAR LORD, Thank you for taking care of all your children. Thank you for being the ultimate parent—the ultimate example of how to serve. Thank you for reminding us that we need to be your children. We need to depend on you.

Please steer us to the ministry where we can serve you best. Open doors and create connections with students that ultimately draw both us and the students closer to you. IN JESUS' NAME, AMEN.

Helpful Hints

- You may find that you love teaching. If you don't enjoy the experience, try again with another age level.
- You might also discover that you are more of a behind-the-scenes person. That's great! Every Sunday school teacher would be incredibly blessed if he or she had someone interested in gathering supplies, preparing snacks, and taking care of all the other details that go into a Sunday school program.
- Students in middle school and high school can be extra sensitive to their parents' presence in a social setting. If you have a desire to serve with adolescents and have a child that age, ask your child first. If he or she prefers that you are *not* involved with the ministry he or she attends, pick another age level or ask the youth pastor if you can help out in a behind-the-scenes manner. Allow your children the space in ministry—a healthy environment—to navigate the thick and mucky waters of adolescence…without their own parents watching.

Reflect

- What did you learn from the children or the students?
- What were the enjoyable parts of this experience? What would you never want to do again?
- Jesus made the ultimate sacrifice of love to serve you. What might he be calling you to sacrifice as you are serving others?

A Talent to Serve

Ask everyone in your group to consider what his or her interests and talents are. For example, one person may be an expert gardener while another is a talented flutist. Have each person prayerfully come up with a strategic plan for how he or she could build up the church by leading in that specific area of expertise. For example, an expert gardener could put together a team to plant a church vegetable garden and then donate all the produce to a homeless shelter; a talented flutist might offer free or discounted lessons to children in the congregation and then put on a church concert every six months.

> "Are we all apostles? Are we all prophets? Are we all teachers? Do we all have the power to do miracles? Do we all have the gift of healing? Do we all have the ability to speak in unknown languages? Do we all have the ability to interpret unknown languages? Of course not! So you should earnestly desire the most helpful gifts" (1 Corinthians 12:29-31a).

Be as detail-oriented and as practical as possible. Then have each person present his or her plan to the rest of the group. Does anyone feel particularly passionate about his or her plan? Encourage each other to put your plans in action if you feel God leading you in that direction.

Dear Jesus, Thank you for creating such a diverse and beautiful church. Thank you for giving people unique and creative talents. Thank you for using these talents to serve you, the church, and the world. Forgive us when we ignore a need.

Please guide us, as a group, to serve you well as the body of Christ—all serving you in ways that you have specifically and intentionally intended for us. Help us be accepting when others offer to serve us. In Jesus' name, amen.

Reflect

- What did you discover about yourself?
- How does your passion or talent fit in your church body?
- How can you serve your family and close friends with the talents God has given you?
- How can you serve at work or in the community with that same talent?

Helpful Hints

- There may already be a ministry in your church that could use your talent. Check with the people who lead that ministry and see where they could use your talent.

Janitor's Day Off

"We are confident of all this because of our great trust in God through Christ. It is not that we think we are qualified to do anything on our own. Our qualification comes from God" (2 Corinthians 3:4-6).

Church janitors work very long hours, often logging a lot of evening and weekend overtime. Their work is hard and often goes unrecognized. Organize your group to give your janitor or janitors a much-deserved day off.

Talk to the person who supervises the janitor(s) at your church, and ask what day would be easiest for your crew to take over. Get a list of daily janitorial duties, and note where all the supplies are kept. Then have volunteers sign up for one- to two-hour shifts, enough to make up a full eight-hour day. Assign duties from the list to each shift. Some will need to be repeated each shift, such as emptying the trash cans and checking the bathrooms for toilet paper and paper towels.

While you might want to surprise the janitor with his or her day off, give advance notice so he or she can plan activities for the day and make notes for your volunteer janitors.

Dear God, Thank you for the facility you have given our church. Thank you for the people who serve by taking care of it.

Please make us more aware of the tracks that we're leaving, and help us be more conscious to serve the janitorial staff and other people at the church— ultimately serving you—by taking note of our own surroundings.

Help those who work so hard in cleaning our church to use this unexpected free time to rest or do something they truly enjoy. In Jesus' name, amen.

Helpful Hints

- Partner with those leading large-group events, and offer to do a "clean sweep" directly following the big program. Empty the trash, pick up any items that belong in the lost-and-found, vacuum, return furniture to its original location, clean off chalk- or dry-erase boards, and so on. That way, when the janitors arrive, they are pleasantly surprised by the easy job ahead.

Reflect

- What did you notice about the meeting area and how people leave the church building after participating in a program? How did this day of service affect your perspective on keeping the church clean?
- How well do you know those who serve "behind the scenes" at church?

Orphans and Widows

In the early church, "orphans and widows" needed to be protected, as they were outside the protective boundaries of a family unit. In our society, elderly people often lack family nearby to help care for them and their needs. As a group, adopt an elderly individual (or couple).

"Pure and genuine religion in the sight of God the Father means caring for orphans and widows in their distress and refusing to let the world corrupt you" (James 1:27).

The person could be a member of your church or someone who lives near the church. Try to choose someone who is unable to get around very well, who needs some help and companionship. Look for someone who doesn't have a lot of family in the area.

Throughout the year, provide services for your adopted senior, such as mowing the grass, raking leaves, or shoveling snow. There may be other services you can provide inside the house, such as moving furniture or doing any cleaning the senior is unable to do alone. You can also plant flowers, bake cookies, or prepare a meal. Some members of your group could volunteer to be on call to take your adopted senior to the doctor or church or to run errands.

Don't get so wrapped up in chores, however, that you forget the aspect of companionship. Encourage your volunteers to take time out from raking to strike up a conversation with your adopted senior. Make sure to send birthday and holiday cards and stop by for periodic visits.

DEAR GOD, Thank you for creating those who are at different places in life. Please help me take on your heart of servanthood and to reach out to those who could use a hand. Open my mind and my eyes to what I can learn from people who have lived so much life. Thank you for the privilege of interacting with people from another generation. IN JESUS' NAME, AMEN.

Reflect

• Why do you think that the tradition of caring for the elderly has been lost in our culture?
• Who takes care of the elderly people who are important in your life?
• What has been the most fun part of this experience?

Helpful Hints

• If your group is large, adopt more than one senior.
• Get to know the person's family when they are in town visiting.
• Ask before you decide to adopt someone. Your good intentions might be perceived as being nosy or pushy.
• If the person lives alone, package meals in individual servings. That way, they can easily go from the freezer to microwave to table.

Serving Your
SMALL GROUP

It's easy to think of serving as something you do for others *outside your group*. But serving should be done internally as well. How do you carry one another's burdens? How do you build up one another? How do you wash each other's feet (literally and metaphorically)?

Making intentional efforts to serve one another will build up your group and make it stronger. Your relationships will grow stronger. Your vulnerability with one another will become more natural. Your spiritual impact on one another—and on the world—will be that much greater.

"So Jesus called them together and said, 'You know that the rulers in this world lord it over their people, and officials flaunt their authority over those under them. But among you it will be different. Whoever wants to be a leader among you must be your servant, and whoever wants to be first among you must be the slave of everyone else. For even the Son of Man came not to be served but to serve others and to give his life as a ransom for many.' "

—Mark 10:42-45

Service Scavenger Hunt

"So encourage each other and build each other up, just as you are already doing" (1 Thessalonians 5:11).

Need an activity for a small-group fun night, but putt-putt golf is getting old? Why not have a service scavenger hunt? Group members will go on a hunt to find ways to serve and encourage one another. Here's what you'll do:

At the beginning of the night, have members each write the following information on an index card: favorite way to relax, favorite candy or treat, things that make the person feel loved, favorite music, favorite hobby, and so on. After the cards are filled out, put them in a hat, and have each member pick one. Then have members get in teams of two.

The teams will be sent on their way to hunt together for ways to serve, bless, or encourage the people whose cards they got. (Make sure team members don't have one another's cards.) For example, if a member's favorite way to relax is in a bubble bath, buy some bath salts. If the favorite candy listed is Snickers, buy a bar.

But there are other ways to serve besides the material. If a member prizes his or her truck greatly, sneak to that person's house and give it a wash. If a member loves golf, give an IOU or a gift certificate for a round together.

Gather back together after about an hour and a half to give your gifts of service and encouragement to one another.

DEAR LORD, Thank you for giving us one another to experience your kind of community together. Help us to encourage one another and build one another up. We want to have relationships that honor and glorify you. IN JESUS' NAME, AMEN.

Helpful Hints

- Make sure to remind your small group why you're doing what you're doing—loving, encouraging, and serving one another is what you're called to do!
- You may want to set a budget limit at the beginning of the evening—let members know they should keep the costs for their service within a range.

Reflect

- Read 1 Thessalonians 5:11. How do you think we're doing as a small group in encouraging one another?
- How did it feel to be served tonight? How did it feel to serve others?
- What can we practically do to improve our loving and serving one another?

The Great Child Exchange

It used to be a dollar an hour, if that. But now the price of baby-sitting often keeps couples at home.

If your small group includes people with children, pick one Saturday a month, and rotate child-care responsibilities. Give the other parents in the group a chance to go out on the town or enjoy a quiet evening at home. It's a simple exchange that will provide you and your spouse a child-free evening almost every month—every month except the one when it's your turn.

If your small group is child-free, pick another small group who has children, and offer this service once every other month. This might not seem like very often or a big deal, but to the parents who are receiving free and safe child care every eight weeks, it is a huge service.

Dear God, Thank you for the precious gift of children. Thank you for the families who raise them. Please help us be patient and learn how to play again. Remind us what it's like to be a child as we spend time with a group of kids. Please help us be creative in the way we care for the youngest of your creation. Thank you for the opportunity to see life through all these children's eyes. In Jesus' name, amen.

Reflect

- What is one thing that you learned from a child?
- What and how can you be praying for a specific child or family?

"Then Jesus called for the children and said to the disciples, 'Let the children come to me. Don't stop them! For the Kingdom of God belongs to those who are like these children. I tell you the truth, anyone who doesn't receive the Kingdom of God like a child will never enter it' " (Luke 18:16-17).

Helpful Hints

- Make sure that you have the appropriate facilities to handle the children. If there are young ones, take precautions to childproof the house where everyone is meeting. You could also ask your church if it's OK to use their facilities.
- Plan theme nights for children, such as a movie-and-popcorn night, game night, or jungle night. This will give kids something to anticipate.
- Get a few children's books from the library. They're free!
- Ask ahead of time about food allergies before serving any snacks.
- If the number of children is overwhelming for one couple or your small group, have couples double up for the night or invite some friends.
- Bedtime is a challenge, and taking home sleeping children can be difficult, so try to make it an early night.

38

Pick a Name

"Don't worry about anything; instead, pray about everything. Tell God what you need, and thank him for all he has done" (Philippians 4:6).

It's easy to serve your own small-group members—just ask how each member would like to be served!

At any given small-group meeting time, distribute small pieces of paper to each member (make sure to include yourself). Ask group members to write on the paper one way an individual could best serve them at this time. This could be anything from: "I need a ride on Monday" to "My computer is not working right now."

Ask each member to write his or her name on the bottom of the paper, fold it up, and place it in a hat. One by one, each member will draw a slip of paper. Now it's up to everyone to come up with the best way to serve the owner of the paper!

DEAR GOD, Thank you for blessing us with this small group. Thank you for the individuals who are on this team and the unique gifts they bring to our fellowship. I ask that you would give insight and love to each of us as we seek to serve our fellow teammates. IN JESUS' NAME, AMEN.

Reflect

- How did you feel writing your need on the piece of paper?
- Do you find it more difficult to serve or be served? Why?
- How did serving each other differ from serving strangers?

Helpful Hints

- You may find that some individuals are more suited to certain needs. In this case, you may elect to allow people to swap papers in order to best serve each member.
- Set a time limit for the service ideas. Ask people to serve one another at some point this week or month.

Honey-Do Wish List

Have each person in the group identify one or two "honey-do" type of jobs at home that just haven't gotten done but would be a real blessing to have completed. These could be anything from removing a dead tree or shrub to cleaning and organizing a closet or work space, to weeding and planting a garden area, painting a room, or fixing a broken fence or door.

"So now I am giving you a new commandment: Love each other. Just as I have loved you, you should love each other. Your love for one another will prove to the world that you are my disciples" (John 13:34-35).

Determine how much time the group will spend at each home. Then review and agree on what one job the group could do for each member. Determine what will be required to accomplish each task and how much can be done in the allotted time, and plan how it will be achieved.

Then make a schedule for the group to go to each person's home and work together to accomplish the task. You might want to set aside two hours per week for several weeks and go to one home per week. Or perhaps do one job a month, or take a Saturday or two and plow through several projects in a day.

DEAR LORD OF LOVE, Help us to realize more fully that we are family. And help us to love the members in this family of God as you love them. As we show our love through practical ways, by laboring for one another, help our love for each other to grow, and in doing so, prove to others that we are your disciples. IN JESUS' NAME, AMEN.

Reflect

- When Jesus told us to love one another, he wasn't just talking about having fond feelings for one another. What was he talking about?
- How did this project challenge or grow your love for people in the group?
- How will you continue showing love to others even after these projects are completed?

Helpful Hints

- Have each group member purchase ahead of time any supplies or materials necessary for his or her job.
- If there is some prep work that a member can do to facilitate a project once the crew arrives, complete that ahead of time to better use everyone's time.
- If a work project will extend over a meal time, plan a break ahead of time so that everyone can disperse and find a bite to eat. Or have everyone brown-bag it and eat together, or order in from a restaurant and share the expense.

40 Day Cook-Off

"All the believers were united in heart and mind. And they felt that what they owned was not their own, so they shared everything they had" (Acts 4:32).

Plan a day for a cook-off! Cook together and make meals, sharing your favorite recipes. After the cook-off, everyone will have an entree of each person's favorite recipe.

Everyone should choose his or her favorite entree and obtain the recipe. Don't worry if you're no cook. If you dislike cooking or your Midas touch around the stove is more burnt char than gold, rely on the expertise of others while enjoying the fellowship of the group. Besides, you can always wash dishes or chop celery!

Buy enough ingredients to make as many batches of your recipe as there are people in the group. Provide zipper storage bags or disposable pans and foil to contain your entree once cooked.

Choose a location to cook—someone's home with a spacious kitchen or a church facility, if available. Confirm what cookware will be available at the chosen kitchen, and take along any extra supplies you'll need. Coordinate items such as spices so there aren't six new jars of garlic salt with a teaspoon used from each.

Cook away! Divide the tasks to use the space and time as efficiently as possible. Once the meals are prepared and in their containers, swap them so that everyone has a variety of different meals to take home. Write on the bag or foil with a permanent marker any special instructions for storage or use. Freeze what you can, and use in the following week what won't freeze well.

DEAR PROVIDER, Thank you for the food you give us. Thank you for the abundance and variety, so that eating is not just a necessity but a pleasure. Help us to be united as we prepare our meals together. IN JESUS' NAME, AMEN.

Helpful Hints

- For each recipe, calculate the cost of ingredients. Then determine how to split the expenses.
- Even if someone dislikes cooking, encourage his or her participation with such things as organizing the cook-off, purchasing ingredients, or keeping equipment and work areas clean as the cooking progresses.

Reflect

- The Bible tells of Jesus sharing many meals with others. Why do you think Jesus' eating with others was important enough to record?
- How does serving one another help make you "united in heart and mind"?
- Why does God want you to be "united in heart and mind"?

Cruising Around

Cars. We all have them. We all need them. For many of us, they're one of the biggest investments we have. And yet most of us forget about them within a minute of turning them off. At least until something goes wrong. Why not show some practical love to your fellow group members by giving each other's cars the kind of care they deserve (and very likely need)?

> "Is there any encouragement from belonging to Christ? Any comfort from his love? Any fellowship together in the Spirit? Are your hearts tender and compassionate? Then make me truly happy by agreeing wholeheartedly with each other, loving one another, and working together with one mind and purpose" (Philippians 2:1-2).

Take a day to go from group member's home to group member's home and show each other's cars some love. Everyone can have a hand helping out. The more car-savvy members of your group can do oil changes or radiator flushes, or at least check all the fluid levels (and take a run to the auto shop if someone needs a top-off). Oil, transmission, brakes, steering, and radiator are all possibilities, depending on the year and make of car.

Those who don't know their filters from their fenders can wash the cars, clean the inside windows, or vacuum the carpets. Even if the new-car smell's long gone, you can help each other rediscover that new-car *feel*.

As you go from house to house, use the opportunity to make a conversational meal out of it. With a little bit of advance planning, you could arrange to have different foods and refreshments at each home where you stop. Have a bigger celebration at your last stop, and take time to appreciate the work you've done for each other.

DEAR LORD, Bless our time together as a group today, as we help each other to take care of the blessings you've already given us in these vehicles we use each day. Help us to work together, have fun together, serve each other as we would serve you, and celebrate our time together as a group. IN JESUS' NAME, AMEN.

Reflect

- What was it like to help your fellow group members in a practical way?
- How has this activity given you a greater appreciation for the things you own? for each other as a group?
- How could you help other friends and neighbors in a way similar to this?

Helpful Hints
- Go to the auto store beforehand and buy things in cheaper bulk quantities, depending on what needs are.

Mother's Day Dinner

> "In the same way, husbands ought to love their wives as they love their own bodies. For a man who loves his wife actually shows love for himself. No one hates his own body but feeds and cares for it, just as Christ cares for the church...'Honor your father and mother.' This is the first commandment with a promise: If you honor your father and mother, 'things will go well for you, and you will have a long life on the earth' " (Ephesians 5:28-29; 6:2-3).

Have the men in your small group plan a Mother's Day dinner for the special women in their lives. Plan it either for your regular group night or on Mother's Day Sunday. (If one half of your couples don't normally come to group, this is a great opportunity to get those people involved as well.) If your group likes, you could easily turn this into a multigenerational celebration—get the kids involved with helping; invite the grandparents and honor them as well. Even invite neighbors who don't come to group to be part of the fun, if you like.

But make sure the dads or husbands are in charge. This is an opportunity for them to use their creative abilities, and exercise their administrative abilities as well. Let one of your men pull the plan together and get everything assigned. There's probably at least one cook—let him have at it. Buy flowers—hey, it's Mother's Day. If one of your men is particularly gifted with video software, let him create a video or slide show of the wives and mothers you're honoring. It could be a very powerful time watching it together at the end of your evening.

DEAR LORD, We thank you for our wives (and mothers). We love them, and we honor them as you have called us to do tonight. Help them to know how much we appreciate them, even when we're not as good at expressing it as we should be. Help us in expressing that better in the future as well. Help them to feel honored tonight, both by us and by you. IN JESUS' NAME, AMEN.

Helpful Hints

- Throw in some games, too, if you like. One fun idea would be to take turns blindfolding Mom, let everyone shout at once, and have her try to find her "child" amidst the din (even if it's the child she married!).
- Let the men have a cake-decorating contest. You'll either discover some hidden artistic abilities or have a good laugh watching the guys reinforce what you may have already expected!

Reflect

- (Men) What abilities did you discover about yourselves or each other as you worked together on this evening?
- (Women) What was the most special thing about tonight for you?
- (Men and Kids) What are some ways you can honor and show appreciation for your wives and moms during the rest of the year?

Party Packages

Themed gift baskets are fun to make and even more fun to receive. So honor each member of your small group with a specialty gift basket based on a particular love, be it gardening, Italian cooking, movies, or fishing.

"For God knew his people in advance, and he chose them to become like his Son, so that his Son would be the firstborn among many brothers and sisters" (Romans 8:29).

If your group is just starting out together, finding out more about each other's interests would be a nice icebreaker. If you've been together for a while, you probably already know what kind of basket would please each member.

Decide how you'll go about delivering the baskets. You might draw names and each person will prepare a basket for the person he or she drew. Or you might draw names and work in pairs or teams. Or you might have a committee that surprises different members with baskets each month.

Bear in mind, though, that you don't have to use actual *baskets*. A fishing theme might be housed in a bucket or fishing creel and contain lures, hooks, bait, maps, fishing line, a reel, and a ruler for good measure. An Italian cooking theme could be housed in a pasta pot or colander. A movie-theme container could be an unused popcorn tub.

Once you start, you'll have no shortage of ideas—and no shortage of fun when your small-group members receive their gifts.

Dear Lord, Thank you for the people in our small group. Thank you for providing our time of fellowship and learning. Help us to honor each other. In Jesus' name, amen.

Reflect

- What surprised you about the diversity of interests in your small group?
- What does that say about God's creativity?
- How did this service project help you become closer to members of your small group?

Helpful Hints

- Your gift baskets don't have to be expensive, just thoughtful. Make them as small as you'd like. Even a few specialty tea bags in a pretty cup would delight a tea lover.
- This service project is a way of honoring the members of your small group. Resist the urge to include gag gifts in your baskets.

Talent Teaching

"The human body has many parts, but the many parts make up one whole body. So it is with the body of Christ" (1 Corinthians 12:12).

Each member of your small group has a special talent or gift to share. Maybe one person is an expert fly fisherman who ties her own flies. Maybe another makes the best carrot cake on earth. Maybe another plays the piano well.

Host a talent night not only to showcase one another's talents, but to *share* them as well. Here's how it works: Each person will prepare a short demonstration of his or her talent. If people protest that they have no talents, work together as a group to think of talents each person could share. Make it a time of honoring and building each other up.

In addition to the talent demonstration, each person should come up with a way to share that talent with the group as a way of thanking everyone for the friendship throughout the year. For example, the person who fly fishes could give a fly-casting demonstration then give each person in the group a hand-tied fly as a reminder of their fellowship together. The person who plays the piano could play a selection then give each person a CD of favorite piano music.

At the end of the evening, each person will have reminders from the rest of the group. Close the meeting in prayer, thanking God for the special talents and abilities he gives each of his children. Encourage group members to thank God for their small group each time they look at one of the reminders.

DEAR LORD, Thank you for the special talents you've given each member of our small group. Thank you for their willingness to share those talents with each other. Please help us to be mindful of how special each person you put in our lives is. IN JESUS' NAME, AMEN.

Helpful Hints

- If you have a large group, you may want to host a special long meeting, break this project into two nights, or set a time limit for each presentation.
- If you have new people, shy people, or people who insist they have no talents to share, let them work in teams.

Reflect

- What did you learn about the members of your small group through this?
- How is sharing your time and talent a way of showing God's love?
- How will the reminders you received help you honor your small-group members in the weeks to come?

Birthday Buddies

Have everyone in your group put his or her name and birthday on a piece of paper. Collect the papers, and put them in a hat. Have everyone draw one name (be sure no one gets a spouse's name).

> "He makes the whole body fit together perfectly. As each part does its own special work, it helps the other parts grow, so that the whole body is healthy and growing and full of love" (Ephesians 4:16).

Let people know that it's now their responsibility to coordinate small-group birthday celebrations for the person whose name they drew. Encourage people to plan the birthday events according to the person's likes: hobbies, restaurants, movies, themes... the possibilities are endless! Remind people that even though they are to *coordinate* the celebrations, that doesn't mean the responsibility is solely theirs. They can recruit other people in the group to help with parts of the celebrations as well.

By divvying up celebrations this way, you can ensure that each birthday celebration is unique and special...and that the responsibility for coordinating those celebrations doesn't always fall on the same person.

Dear God, Thank you so much for creating the people in our group. We are so grateful for each one of them. Help us celebrate their births together, as well as the wonderful ways you've used each of them to bring joy and purpose to our group. In Jesus' name, amen.

Reflect

- How does it feel to be in charge of planning someone's birthday?
- How can you make that person's birthday super-special?
- How can celebrating someone's birthday give you a deeper appreciation of that person and God's plan for his or her life?

Helpful Hints

- Coordinate with the person's spouse or family to plan an even larger birthday celebration!
- Don't feel like you have to keep every party a surprise. Some people may prefer to help plan their own party...or at least to know what's going on.

Serving Your
FRIENDS AND FAMILY

Laying down your life...it sounds so noble and glorious. And most of us would say—without hesitation—that we'd die for a friend or a family member.

But laying down your life isn't always about *dying* for someone. There are other ways to give your life for your friends and family. Not-so-glorious ways, small ways, *everyday* ways.

You could lay down your life by baby-sitting for your sister on a Friday night. You could lay down your life by helping your friend clean out the garage, by taking your brother's hockey stick and getting it fixed for him, by sacrificing your own Saturday to go with a friend to visit her mother in the nursing home...

Laying down your life and *serving* your friends and family members may not always seem noble or glorious. But it's what a committed relationship is all about.

"This is my commandment: Love each other in the same way I have loved you. There is no greater love than to lay down one's life for one's friends. You are my friends if you do what I command. I no longer call you slaves, because a master doesn't confide in his slaves. Now you are my friends, since I have told you everything the Father told me. You didn't choose me. I chose you. I appointed you to go and produce lasting fruit, so that the Father will give you whatever you ask for, using my name. This is my command: Love each other."

—John 15:12-17

Small-Group Garden

"The Lord will guide you continually, giving you water when you are dry and restoring your strength. You will be like a well-watered garden, like an ever-flowing spring" (Isaiah 58:11).

Here's a great way for all the green thumbs out there to serve friends and family while bonding as a small group: Start a small-group garden. Go to your city's home page to find out if there is a community garden you can reserve a plot in, see if your church can spare a corner lot for a garden, or agree upon a small and accessible plot in a small-group member's yard.

Agree to use the bounty of your garden to bless your family and friends. And make it a group effort! Decide together what you want to plant: flowers to give as surprises to spouses or friends who need cheering, or maybe vegetables and herbs to give as a culinary delight to unsuspecting friends. Form teams to buy the seeds or plants together, to plant them together, to tend them together, and to harvest them together. (Key word: *together!*)

Create a rotating schedule for tending the garden in pairs. You don't want all the work to fall on one or two people or it will become a burden. Communicate at small group each week what's ready for picking, and plan how to use it best.

Maybe some small-group members are better cooks than gardeners. They can create salads and meals with the produce to serve to loved ones. They can provide dishes for families who just had a baby, who have illnesses, or who just need a treat.

DEAR LORD, Thank you for giving us this garden to tend. We pray that working it together would bond us in a special way. Thank you for the way you bless us through something as simple as a garden, and we pray our small gifts to others would cheer them and be a reflection of your kindness. IN JESUS' NAME, AMEN.

Reflect

- Tell about one person who was blessed through our garden.
- What's one way you grew closer to someone in the small group from working on the garden together?
- Read Isaiah 58:11. How are we like this thriving garden when God is our light and water?

Helpful Hints

- You never know how big your garden will grow. If you have extra produce, by all means take it to a local soup kitchen!
- Begin planning your garden in early spring so you can plant in May.

It's All in the Detail!

As Christians, we can get caught up in serving to fulfill a purpose, to meet a specific need… if someone is hungry, we feed the person; if someone needs clothing, we give the person a jacket. Sometimes, serving can be implemented to treat those we love to a well-deserved break! As a small group, choose a relative or friend of one of your group members. You can choose someone who is going through a tough time or

"Is there any encouragement from belonging to Christ? Any comfort from his love? Any fellowship together in the Spirit? Are your hearts tender and compassionate? Then make me truly happy by agreeing wholeheartedly with each other, loving one another, and working together with one mind and purpose" (Philippians 2:1-2).

simply select an individual who would really appreciate an auto detail! On a day that is mutually convenient, take this person's vehicle for three or four hours. As a team, scrub it until it shines. Wash it, wax it, clean the tires, vacuum it, wipe the dash, shake out the mats, clean the windows, and scrape every bug off the front grill, returning it with a full tank of gas. Now that's service!

DEAR GOD, We thank you for the small things in our lives that go unnoticed. Thank you for food in the fridge, friends close by, and a functioning automobile. We want to thank you for these and other small blessings. Please bless the owner of this vehicle today! IN JESUS' NAME, AMEN.

Reflect

- Did this person react to his or her freshly detailed car as you expected? In what way?
- What did you think about during the cleaning of the vehicle?
- How do you imagine God was honored through this service?

Helpful Hints

- As a group, you may choose to include other vehicle services as the situation requires, such as oil changes, fluid top-offs, and wheel rotations.
- Whatever you do, make sure that the vehicle looks great when you return it! There's no point in taking someone's car if you're going to do a sub-standard job.
- If you have time, consider doing the same service for even more people!

Get the Gear Back in the Game

"Your love has given me much joy and comfort, my brother, for your kindness has often refreshed the hearts of God's people" (Philemon 1:7).

Have you ever found yourself admiring the activities of a family member whose interests are completely different from your own? Or perhaps you're grateful that you're able to share the outdoor events you enjoy with a friend who also likes them. Have each person in your small group think of a specific person and that person's favorite fitness-related activity...

You're going to refresh and repair your loved one's sports gear! Eligible equipment could include golf clubs, rock-climbing gear, bicycles, fishing tackle, baseball gloves, canoes or kayaks, camping gear, or hockey equipment.

Arrange to pick up the sports paraphernalia from your friend or family member ahead of time—you can tell the person what you're planning to do with it or leave the planned outcome a surprise. Then, either take the gear to a reputable service shop and pay for the necessary restoration and repairs or refresh the equipment yourself if you know the proper procedures and have the correct tools.

Return the refurbished sports gear to the fortunate recipient with a note that says something similar to this: "I admire your devotion to [this sport]. I hope this gift of restoration will bring you more refreshing enjoyment."

DEAR LORD, *Thank you for creating our family and friends with unique interests. Thank you for the opportunity for us to serve them and show them we care about their happiness and safety by caring for their sports gear.* IN JESUS' NAME, AMEN.

Helpful Hints

- If taking the gear into a service shop, call or ask around first to find the location with the most highly regarded reputation.
- When you return the gear, include the contact information of the service shop or technician who did the work so that your friend can take the equipment back to the same place for additional repairs in the future.

Reflect

- What kind of impact did your act of service have on your friend or family member?
- How do you think God can work through people while they are enjoying their favorite outdoor activities? How have you seen God work through you or your friends in this manner?

Third Place

God very specifically calls us to love him. It's much easier said than done. If it were natural for sinful people to love God as their first priority, God probably wouldn't have to say it over

> **"And you must love the Lord your God with all your heart, all your soul, and all your strength" (Deuteronomy 6:5).**

and over and over again and again and again all throughout Scripture. God also calls us—and has to remind us—to love others. It's so much easier and oftentimes more comfortable to think of "me" first, before God and before others.

Pick a friend or family member you see and interact with on a regular basis, preferably almost daily. What are your interactions like? What are his or her needs? Make a commitment with the others in your small group to intentionally think of this friend's needs before yours. It may mean going out of your way to drive to the airport or help with laundry. It might mean learning to intentionally listen or pray for the person daily.

First, spend a week writing down service opportunities. Try to take at least a few minutes every day to think about what this person's expressed or unexpressed needs are. At the end of the week, present these ideas to your small group. For the next month, try to meet one of those needs at least every other day. Third place is a good place to be.

After about a month, get together with your small group to discuss and debrief the experience.

DEAR GOD, Thank you for setting an example of how to serve. Please forgive us for the times that we've pushed our way to first place. Teach us to think of you first, others second, and ourselves third. IN JESUS' NAME, AMEN.

Reflect

- How is it easy for you to serve this person?
- What are the needs you notice that are most challenging to meet?
- How have you started noticing the needs of other people and put them ahead of yours?

Helpful Hints

- Don't necessarily choose the most helpless person you know. Be creative and challenge yourself to change the way you view people and notice the needs of others.
- If you have non-Christian friends and family members, use this opportunity to share God's love.

50

Free Gym!

"For our dying bodies must be transformed into bodies that will never die; our mortal bodies must be transformed into immortal bodies" (1 Corinthians 15:53).

This project will benefit the health of all involved!

Often many people don't have the finances to join a gym and, for some people, discipline to exercise is hard without external motivation. Put together a group of family members or friends who desire to increase their cardiovascular health, bone strength, and lung capacity through exercise!

With your small group, invite several of your family members and friends to a weekly exercise session. Find a suitable time that works for all participants—but don't worry about children's schedules or baby-sitting, because part of this project involves shared child care. Determine what the average fitness level is of the group, and decide what sorts of exercise you could participate in based upon your climate, location, and so on. At the very least, you can gather to walk together—two to three miles a session, perhaps. If one person is a trained fitness instructor (aerobics, Pilates, dance), ask permission to use a room of your church to exercise during the building's "slow times."

Once you've determined the who, what, when, and where, begin to meet. Using a different volunteer every week, delegate one person to take care of the children (if any).

DEAR GOD, *The psalmist declared himself "fearfully and wonderfully made" (NLT). Through this exercise, may we be good stewards of the bodies you've given us. Take away discontent we have, and comfort us in our physical disappointments.* IN JESUS' NAME, AMEN.

Helpful Hints

- Don't worry about getting a large group for this project; a group of three to five people will be plenty.
- Be sensitive to people's preferences as you plan. Some people would prefer to exercise in single-gender (not co-ed) groups. Others may have physical problems that only allow them to participate in specific activities.

Reflect

- How does exercising with others change your relationship with them?
- How were the participants encouraged by this activity?
- What sorts of things did you learn from one another?

Secret Service

This next service project is anything but mission impossible. Here's how it works: Each small group member will choose one family member or friend to serve for one week. The catch is, the person you're serving *can't* know who is serving—it has to be done in secret.

"But when you give to someone in need, don't let your left hand know what your right hand is doing. Give your gifts in private, and your Father, who sees everything, will reward you" (Matthew 6:3-4).

OK, so this sounds a little bit like secret Santa, but there's a twist with this version—Secret Service—in that your focus should not be on giving physical gifts, but showing Christ's love by serving.

Here are a few ways you might serve people:

• Wash their cars, mow their lawns, or clean out their gutters;
• Cook them meals or pack them lunches;
• Send encouraging notes or cards each day;
• Write down your prayers for them and mail them each day; or
• Send someone on a "secret service" mission to do something on your behalf. This is a great idea for those service ideas you have that require interaction with the person you want to serve.

Dear Jesus, Help us to always be on a mission for you. Speak to us and show us those we can serve around us on a daily basis. In your name, amen.

Reflect

• How did it feel to serve others in secret rather than in the open?
• Was it easy or difficult to be secretive? Did you get caught?
• How did God work through you during this project? How did God speak to you or meet a need of yours?

Helpful Hints

• Pray for the person before you begin serving. Ask God to show you specific things you can do to serve.

• After your week of service is complete, throw a dinner or grill out. Have everyone who participated share a meal, and then reveal your secret identities.

• Come up with ideas for service during your small-group meeting—that way you can all benefit from one another's creativity!

• If there are kids in your small group, get them involved as well!

Encouragement Works

"One of the things I always pray for is the opportunity, God willing, to come at last to see you. For I long to visit you so I can bring you some spiritual gift that will help you grow strong in the Lord. When we get together, I want to encourage you in your faith, but I also want to be encouraged by yours" (Romans 1:10-12).

Encouragement ultimately has to do with challenging people to a deeper walk with God. As a small group, think and pray about the family members and friends God has placed in each of your lives. Each person should identify one family member or friend with whom he or she could work to develop a close encouraging relationship. Determine where this person is in his or her faith journey. Is this person skeptical, investigating the faith, a new believer, reconnecting with the church, or a seasoned veteran of the faith?

Encourage small-group members to each invite that person out for coffee or ice cream this week and talk about whether the person would be willing to enter into such a relationship. Suggest that small-group members meet with these friends or family members weekly for a period of four to six weeks to simply talk about their relationships with God.

Dear Lord, You are a God of encouragement. Help us to encourage one another through your words and through the gifts you've given us. Pair the right people together that their faiths might grow as they regularly meet together. In Jesus' name, amen.

Helpful Hints

- Be a good friend. Establish a foundation of love and care before ever expecting an opportunity to talk about spiritual things.
- Have realistic expectations. Don't expect this person to be like you or to have the same passion for God that you do. And don't seek to change him or her or be dictating. Your role is to be a loving encourager.
- Be a good listener. Show you care by taking interest.
- Keep the meetings casual. Between meetings touch base with the person. Use notes, phone calls, and e-mail.
- Don't forget to pray about this relationship regularly.

Reflect

- How did this relationship affect your personal faith and spiritual journey?
- How were you an encourager? How were you encouraged?
- How will you continue growing this relationship?

Drive-Through Service

Most everyone loves fast food. Why? Because it's fast. This project is all about serving one family in your small group each week. If your small group rotates homes each week, this project is perfect for you. If you don't, well…you might want to think about switching things around for this service idea—it's totally worth it!

"We know what real love is because Jesus gave up his life for us. So we also ought to give up our lives for our brothers and sisters" (1 John 3:16).

Here's how it goes: To start, take a calendar to your next small-group meeting, and talk about when everyone can meet. Set up your schedule so that everyone gets a chance to host small group for one night. When you have your schedule in place, it's time to get started.

Your small group will meet as normal and go through your regular routine. Instead of mingling over coffee after your get-together each week, you'll go to work on projects that the small-group host family would appreciate. Projects such as:

- Scrubbing the toilets and doing the dishes;
- Dusting, mopping, or washing the baseboards;
- Organizing, sweeping, or the ever-popular folding laundry.

Here's the catch, and why this service project is titled "Drive-Through Service"—you can only spend 25 minutes cleaning. It's quick, fast-paced, down-and-dirty service work.

LORD, You are so good. Thanks for our families, our friends, and most of all for you. You gave yourself up completely—help us do the same each day for each other. IN YOUR NAME, AMEN.

Reflect

- What was it like asking your small group to clean or pick up something at your house?
- Did you notice anyone go out of his or her way to go above and beyond what was expected for this service project?

Helpful Hints

- Each week the list of chores should be challenging, but not impossible. You want your small group to use all 25 minutes, but you also want to make sure no one feels overwhelmed.
- You might think about e-mailing your list of chores ahead of time so small-group members can come prepared to get down to business when it's time to clean.

Encouragement Post

"So encourage each other and build each other up, just as you are already doing" (1 Thessalonians 5:11).

It's old-fashioned, sure...but everyone still loves receiving a handwritten letter.

Spend your small-group time this week writing letters to your friends and family members. Have everyone bring different supplies to the meeting: stationery, stamps, envelopes, nice pens, maybe someone even has a wax seal!

This service project is all about building others up. So as you write, use your letters to impart encouragement, to write prayers for people, to share ways that they have positively impacted your life. As you write, share your letters with one another, chat, laugh...and just in general enjoy the opportunity to sit down and really focus on encouraging people.

DEAR LORD, Thank you for our friends and families. They are so dear to us. Help us to encourage them through these letters and in the words we speak to them. IN JESUS' NAME, AMEN.

Reflect

- Describe the best letter you ever received.
- How do you think your friends and family members will react when they receive your letters?

Helpful Hints

- If you don't have addresses for everyone, try looking them up online. If you still can't find the addresses, go ahead and hand deliver the notes.
- Think of people close by and far away as you write your letters.

Power Progressive Housecleaning Party

It's cleaning time! Set aside one Saturday this month to have a progressive cleaning party.

Ask each small-group member to find one family member or friend who could use help getting on top of his or her chores and would allow your group to come in and do some power cleaning. Talk to the person about what specifically you can clean for him or her, and make an appointment with the person during your predetermined time frame. This might include cleaning the bathrooms, sweeping and mopping the kitchen, cleaning out a refrigerator, washing dishes and cleaning counters, dusting and vacuuming the living area, picking up a playroom, or folding laundry.

> "Two people are better off than one, for they can help each other succeed. If one person falls, the other can reach out and help. But someone who falls alone is in real trouble" (Ecclesiastes 4:9-10).

Start at the first house with brooms, mops, vacuums, cleaning supplies, or any other needed items, and start cleaning! Move from one house to another, and clean the planned portion of each house. As soon as you finish, go to the next house, and do it all over again.

DEAR GOD, As we work together to serve others, use our efforts to accomplish much. Help us to use the time well. And use our work to bless those for whom we work, so that they might better know your love. Help them to feel that they are not alone, that someone has come alongside them, in your name, to help them up. IN JESUS' NAME, AMEN.

Reflect

- What did you like best about serving others in this way? What did you find most difficult?
- What kinds of emotions or reactions to your care did you witness in the individuals you served?

Helpful Hints

- If your group is large, break into smaller groups and clean at several homes at once.
- Include old toothbrushes in your cleaning supplies. They work great on hard-to-get-to places that need some scrubbing.
- Find friends or family members who will be comfortable with a group of strangers coming in to do their cleaning. Offer to do the work when they are out if they would be more comfortable with that arrangement.

Shish Kebarbecue

"And God will generously provide all you need. Then you will always have everything you need and plenty left over to share with others. As the Scriptures say, 'They share freely and give generously to the poor. Their good deeds will be remembered forever' " (2 Corinthians 9:8-9).

It's time for a barbecue with a twist! No ordinary burgers and dogs for this shindig. Invite family members and friends that you know could use a break from the daily grind, and share a fun, tasty meal and fellowship.

Each group member will bring pre-cut chunks of meat to share, such as chicken or lamb, as well as one or two veggies or fruits that go well on shish kebabs, like cherry tomatoes, sweet peppers, mushrooms, and pineapple. Also, divvy up other items, such as drinks, dessert, plates, cups, and utensils. And be sure someone brings the barbecue sauce and skewers!

Make a buffet-style shish-kebab assembly. Each person chooses and places what he or she wants on skewers. Then squeeze or brush on barbecue sauce, and place them on the grill.

When it's all cooked up, eat up and have a great time of fellowship and feasting. Bring out some board games—those kind where you have to shout and laugh to play—and team up, with a variety of ages per team, so that everyone gets a chance to play.

DEAR GOD IN HEAVEN, Thank you for your provision. Thank you that we can share your blessings with others. Help us to use our barbecue to support those who are poor—poor in spirit, energy, or hope. Show us how we can be more godly and more generous through this barbecue. IN JESUS' NAME, AMEN.

Helpful Hints

- Plan some games to promote good fun and healthy laughter.
- Have different-colored markers available, and put markings on the ends of skewers to identify to whom they belong.
- Include alternatives for vegetarians.
- When inviting others, let them come with empty hands. Communicate to them your purpose in providing a time for relaxation and renewal.

Reflect

- Did anything go surprisingly well for you in this event? Explain.
- How would you describe the greatest challenge?
- How did this event seem to serve those invited to participate?

Free Help Yellow Pages

This service project will establish an ongoing support network for friends and family members who may need assistance in a variety of areas.

> "How wonderful and pleasant it is when brothers live together in harmony! For harmony is as precious as the anointing oil that was poured over Aaron's head, that ran down his beard and onto the border of his robe" (Psalm 133:1-2).

Have a brainstorming session to determine what each member of the group, or the group as a whole, can offer to others. This can include things from sewing hems and buttons to fixing leaky faucets and squeaky doors. Or services like balancing checkbooks or cleaning out closets. Perhaps organizing photographs or helping people move. Write down everything you can think of that you could and would do for others. Keep track of who will do what.

Once the list is made, alphabetize it by subject, just like you'd find it in the Yellow Pages. With each entry, include the name and contact information for the individual(s) who will provide that particular service. Print it on yellow paper if you can, and design a cover with a title and description. Bind the pages together by staples or spirals.

Distribute your Yellow Pages to the family members and friends you think could benefit from an offer of this kind. Explain to them your project and how they can use the resources offered.

DEAR LORD, We want to live together in one accord. And we want to live that out by entering others' lives and embodying harmony in all we do. Show us how to leave our comfortable places and join others on their paths. Help us to exemplify harmony as we spend our time and energy on others. IN JESUS' NAME, AMEN.

Reflect

- How did the individuals invited respond to this project?
- How does it feel to make an open-ended offer of help like this, not knowing how much or how frequently you may be asked to assist someone?
- What do you think will be the most difficult aspect of this project? What will come most easily or naturally to you?

Helpful Hints

- If you wish to limit the time frame in which the offers are available or the number or frequency of uses available to each person, include an expiration date on the cover or the stipulations of redemption, such as one per month or 10 total per person.
- For group offers, list one contact person and have him or her make the necessary arrangements to promote facility and avoid confusion.

Feeding on the Word

"And all the believers met together in one place and shared everything they had... They worshiped together at the Temple each day, met in homes for the Lord's Supper, and shared their meals with great joy and generosity—all the while praising God and enjoying the goodwill of all the people. And each day the Lord added to their fellowship those who were being saved" (Acts 2:44, 46-47).

The idea of sharing meals together as Christians has been around as long as the church itself. But it can also be a way to build relationships with friends and neighbors who don't know Jesus. It can be a fun one-time event, but if it goes really well, it could also be the start of a regular gathering time with those who don't know Jesus but need to.

Pick a cuisine, build an entire dinner and setting around your theme, and extend your invitations—in person when possible. Assign different parts of the meal to different group members, and give them fairly easy-to-follow but tasty recipes.

Be sure to not only have fun with the meal, but with the atmosphere for the dinner. Find some music from the country or region whose food you're enjoying. Make or buy decorations that will remind you of that place.

Even more important than the foods you eat, though, are the relationships you grow. Take time to really listen to other friends, neighbors, or family members you invite to your meal. Don't force conversations; rather, take time for relationships to develop, and let them expand naturally while talking about work, the weekend, and anything else going on in each other's lives.

DEAR LORD, We thank you for the opportunity to provide this meal and share it with others—to be your church to others even in this simple way. Help us to be servants to our friends and neighbors tonight, as well as to listen and develop relationships with them. IN JESUS' NAME, AMEN.

Helpful Hints

- Despite what we said about not forcing conversations, it may be a good idea to have a couple of conversation-starting questions or icebreaker activities in reserve, just in case. Check out HomeBuilders *Warm-Ups and Wrap-Ups: 101 Great Ideas for Small Groups* (Group Publishing, Inc.) for some easy ideas to kick off your time together.
- Extend your invitations about two or three weeks in advance.

Reflect

- Does this look like something you could do regularly as a group? Who could you invite to future dinners?
- What needs were brought up during your time together that you might be able to meet as a group?

Second Parents for a Day

Have each member of your small group identify a child he or she knows who could really use more of an adult presence—such as children who live in a single-parent home, kids whose parents might be going through a divorce, or children who may have a difficult relationship with their parents.

"In the same way, encourage the young men to live wisely. And you yourself must be an example to them by doing good works of every kind" (Titus 2:6-7a).

Take a day as a group, and treat those kids to a fun day of activities. Consider taking them to a ballgame or an amusement park or the mall—whatever will be most appropriate and enjoyable for your particular kids.

Be sure to get their parents' permission first. Be very specific in letting parents know where you'll be and what times you expect to be there—and make a point of keeping to that itinerary to the best of your ability.

Who knows? In some cases, this one-time activity could lead to long-term mentoring relationships by your group members, where they'll commit to pouring their lives into these kids' lives.

DEAR GOD, *Bless our time together with these kids today. Help us to be friends as well as elders to them. Help us to listen to them and to enjoy their company.* IN JESUS' NAME, AMEN.

Reflect

- What was the most fun part of today for you personally? What was the biggest challenge?
- What insights did you gain into these kids' lives?
- Would you be interested in doing something like this again or making a longer-term commitment to one or more of these kids? Explain.

Helpful Hints

- As much as possible, let the kids choose what activities you'll do as you go out together.
- Be sure to bring along plenty of healthy snacks for you and the kids.
- Use discretion when asking parents' permission; don't insult parents by implying that you think they're bad parents and need your "help." Simply offer your time and admit that you know things have been rough lately and you'd like to support them.

60

Picture Perfect

"Remember the wonders he has performed, his miracles, and the rulings he has given" (1 Chronicles 16:12).

If you're like most people, you have photographs sitting in boxes waiting to be put in albums. It's a common complaint: "I *want* to do something with those pictures, I would *enjoy* doing something with those pictures, but I can't seem to find the time!"

As a small group, *make* the time for family members or friends. Host a Picture Perfect meeting where everyone brings the photos he or she needs to do something with. You provide a variety of albums, extra album pages, corner picture holders, fine-tipped markers, colored paper, stickers, and refreshments.

If you have a scrapbooker in your midst, all the better! Let him or her teach your family members and friends the fine art of making a scrapbook. To best serve everyone who will come, have a variety of supplies on hand. You might include scrapbook supplies, albums with plastic sleeves, and old-fashioned albums with black pages and corner holders.

As people work, ask them to relive special moments by sharing with the group one or two of their favorite photos. By the end of the meeting, you'll have created a bond of fellowship *and* have accomplished a nagging job!

DEAR LORD, Thank you for the special moments in our lives, and thank you for the special people we share them with. Help us to always remember your goodness. IN JESUS' NAME, AMEN.

Reflect

- Why is it important to remember the special people and experiences God has given us?

- How did people interact during your Picture Perfect meeting? What experiences did they share?
- What did this project tell you about God's provision and goodness?

Helpful Hints

- If the men in your group want something a little more hands-on, let them make frames for someone's favorite pictures.
- Encourage people to wash their hands before starting the project and to try not to touch the face of their photos. Oil from fingers can mar the image.

Bake-Off

Who among us can resist a homemade cake or pie? OK, maybe *some* can, but those people are in the minority.

Host a bake sale for family members and friends. But in this sale, everything is free! Time your service project for when it will be most helpful. A week before Christmas would be a perfect setting. With all of the preparation that goes into the holidays, baking cookies or other specialty goodies can become more of a chore than a charm.

> "(They)…shared their meals with great joy and generosity–all the while praising God and enjoying the goodwill of all the people" (Acts 2:46c-47a).

With members of your small group, make a list of who will bake what so you don't wind up with all chocolate chip cookies. Decide if you'll bake individually or in teams. Decide how many people you can comfortably invite and where you'll host your "sale." Make fliers or invitations to announce the date and time of your event. On the big day, have plates, napkins, plastic wrap, and liquid refreshments on hand.

After the event, sit back and enjoy a few moments of fellowship with your group members. And enjoy the leftovers…if there are any!

DEAR LORD, *Thank you for giving us good families, good friends, and good food to eat. Thank you for the fellowship you provide.* IN JESUS' NAME, AMEN.

Reflect

- What reactions did you see in the people you served during this project?
- Why do you think it's so meaningful for people to share food together?
- What worked well during this service project? What would you do differently next time?

Helpful Hints

- If you do this service project around Christmas, offer a gift wrapping service as well.
- For extra fun, don't tell your friends or family members that everything is free. Just enjoy the smiles on their faces when they find out!

Scripture Albums

"All Scripture is inspired by God and is useful to teach us what is true and to make us realize what is wrong in our lives" (2 Timothy 3:16a).

God's Word is a powerful tool in our Christian walk. Use it to encourage your small group's family members and friends. Together, make Scripture Albums.

First, decide for whom you'll make the albums, and how many copies you'll need. For example, a member of your small group may have a family member or friend who is struggling with a serious illness, so perhaps you'll work together and make only one album for that person. Or you might make a more generic album, copy the pages, and give as many copies as you want. Or, each person might make an individualized album to give away.

Whatever you decide, work together with your small group to make the Scripture Albums happen. Decide on a look, and purchase the necessary supplies. You might decide to write favorite Scripture references on index cards and insert them into inexpensive mini photo albums. Or you might use calligraphy to write Scriptures in a leather-bound journal. You could even decide to let each person choose a favorite Scripture and write a brief account of a life experience where that reference was instrumental.

Whatever you decide, your Scripture Album will be a blessing to who-ever receives it. You can count on it, because you can always count on God's Word!

DEAR LORD, Thank you for revealing yourself to us in your Word. Help us to cling to your teaching, follow your guidance, and share your Word with others. IN JESUS' NAME, AMEN.

Reflect

- How did this project help you connect more with God's Word?
  - How do you think God might use your project down the road in the lives of its recipients?
  - How can you make God's Word more a part of your life?

Helpful Hints

- Even if you make only one album, keep copies of the pages in case you want to do this service project again.
- If you have an artist or photographer in your group, use drawings or pictures to enhance your album.

An Encouraging Week

Spend a few minutes discussing practical ways to show encouragement to others. Then have each person in the group choose at least one person to purposefully encourage throughout this week. It may be a parent, a spouse, a child, a friend, or a co-worker. You may want to choose several people to encourage. For example, you might choose to encourage someone who lacks confidence, someone who's very dear to you, and someone you dislike. Do or say at least one encouraging thing to each person you choose every day of the week. At the end of the week, talk through your experiences together as a small group.

> "Dear brothers and sisters, I close my letter with these last words: Be joyful. Grow to maturity. Encourage each other. Live in harmony and peace. Then the God of love and peace will be with you" (2 Corinthians 13:11).

DEAR GOD, Help us to remember to encourage one another and to encourage those we love. Fill us with your love and joy so that we are overflowing with it and it affects everyone we meet. IN YOUR NAME, AMEN.

Reflect

- Did the person benefit from or appreciate your encouragement?
- How did your encouragement affect your attitude toward the person?
- Would you like to continue encouraging that person?
- Should you broaden your circle of encouragement?

Helpful Hints

- Be sincere in your encouragements—no one appreciates empty flattery.
- Team up together to give big doses of encouragement to mutual friends; send cards, purchase gift certificates, go to lunch all together.

Serving Special Needs

"He comforts us in all our troubles so that we can comfort others. When they are troubled, we will be able to give them the same comfort God has given us" (2 Corinthians 1:4).

If anyone in your group has a family member or friend with a special-needs child, consider offering the parents an afternoon or evening out once a month. Due to a lack of trained or willing baby sitters, parents of special-needs children are rarely able to go out alone and can often go months without the opportunity.

DEAR GOD, Sometimes we struggle to see your plan in the hardships people go through. Comfort us and give us strength as we face the troubles of this world. And help us to offer that same comfort to others that they may know your love. IN JESUS' NAME, AMEN.

Reflect

- How did you feel about this project before you started? How have your feelings changed now?
- What was the hardest part of this project? What surprised you?
- In what other ways can you support the parents of this special-needs child?

Helpful Hints

- You may need to receive special training, depending on the needs of the child. Coordinate with the parents ahead of time to find out if any additional training is required, or spend time with the parents themselves to learn more about the child's needs.
- Build a relationship with the child. All too often, special-needs kids have few adult relationships outside of their parents.
- Try to schedule your once-a-month night at a regular time. For example, plan on baby-sitting the third Saturday of every month; or call parents one week after your last night of baby-sitting to schedule next month's night out.

Carols and Cookies

This year during the Christmas season, plan a night to go caroling and cookie-delivering to the houses of your friends and family members.

During a small-group meeting sometime in early December, have everyone make a list of friends or family members they'd like to visit and serenade with carols. Compile your list, and work together to create a strategic plan for visiting all the houses. If you have a large list, you may want to visit one or two neighborhoods a night for several nights in a row. Set a date for the event and a meeting spot and time.

Ask everyone to bring a dozen yummy Christmas cookies or other holiday goodies for each of the friends or family members that person chose. That way you'll have enough cookies for everyone you visit. You may also want to have people bring a few extras in case you decide to do some caroling at the neighbors' houses as well!

> "I bring you good news that will bring great joy to all people. The Savior—yes, the Messiah, the Lord—has been born today in Bethlehem, the city of David!" (Luke 2:10b-11).

DEAR GOD, We thank you so much for the birth of your Son—our Savior. Your grace and your love for us are unbelievable. Help us to spread that love and the good news of Jesus' birth to the people we visit tonight. IN JESUS' NAME, AMEN.

Reflect

- How do you feel about tonight's caroling experience?
- How did people respond to your presence as carolers? Why do you think they responded that way?
- Would you want to do this again next year? Why or why not?

Helpful Hints

- Dress for the weather! Wear warm coats, gloves, hats, and appropriate shoes.
- Get together once before the big night to practice your chosen carols.
- Go out for warm hot chocolate after you finish singing, and talk together about the whole experience.

Serving Those With
SPECIFIC NEEDS

It's not always fun. It's rarely glorious. It's often thankless.

And yet there are rewards for serving those in need. Great rewards. A smile from someone who hasn't had much to smile about lately. An opening up, a reaching out from someone who doesn't normally trust. A life story told to you from someone who has lived a long and full life. The knowledge you've made a difference. The possibility you've brought someone that much closer to Jesus.

And then there's the heavenly rewards God promises.

And in the end, you see it *is* glorious. There's more thanks than you imagined. And, yes, there was...you did...well, in fact, you had fun, after all...

"Then [Jesus] turned to his host. 'When you put on a luncheon or a banquet,' he said, 'don't invite your friends, brothers, relatives, and rich neighbors. For they will invite you back, and that will be your only reward. Instead, invite the poor, the crippled, the lame, and the blind. Then at the resurrection of the righteous, God will reward you for inviting those who could not repay you.' "

–Luke 14:12-14

66

A Night Out or a Makeover In

"A cheerful look brings joy to the heart; good news makes for good health" (Proverbs 15:30).

Serving battered women.

Maybe you've seen homeless men wandering the streets, eating at soup kitchens, and sleeping in shelters. But in most communities, there are also lesser-known shelters for women who have had to flee their homes—often due to abuse and often with their children. Often these women left home with little more than the clothes on their backs. While the women in these shelters may form close bonds with each other, sometimes residents can feel closed in.

Contact the director of a shelter in your community, and ask how you might be of service. In order for the women in the shelter to go out (for shopping, bowling, dinner, or whatever you choose to treat them to), another part of your group will need to entertain their children at the shelter. Find out the shelter's standards about child care and background checks, and follow them explicitly. Make sure the kids have a great time, too, with special foods and activities.

Members of your group could also spend an evening with the women in the shelter providing facials, manicures, and hairstyling. In the world of uncertainty in which these women dwell, such pampering is a welcome diversion and encouragement. Again, provide something fun for the kids while the moms are being pampered.

Helpful Hints

- Respect women's wishes if they'd prefer not to be in public places, and try to bring an "evening out" to them.
- Guys—don't go alone. Many of these women will probably feel more comfortable around other women or at least having women in the group.
- Invite the women to church. Don't make a big deal out of putting them on the spot, but allow them the freedom to be a participant in a worship service or Bible study just like anyone else. If they went to a shelter because of leaving an abusive situation, they may not be comfortable going back to their church.

DEAR GOD, *You are the ultimate protector and provider, yet sometimes there is still sin and brokenness that we face every day. Protect these women in this particular shelter. Thank you for the courage it took for some of them to leave dangerous situations. Take care of the children, and put healthy role models in their lives.* IN JESUS' NAME, AMEN.

Reflect

- How did this experience impact you?
- How can your church serve these women on a more regular basis?
- What did you learn about yourself by stepping into this environment?

Grocery Express

Serving the elderly.

In the old days, elderly folks could call up their favorite grocery stores, dictate a list of groceries,

"Take care of any widow who has no one else to care for her" (1 Timothy 5:3).

and have them delivered to their front doors. Such days are long gone. As mobility declines, simply obtaining food for the week becomes more and more of a challenge.

There might be people within your own church or community who can use help with grocery shopping. Some people may just need transportation to get to the market and back. Others may feel overwhelmed by the whole situation and may desire someone else to do their shopping for them.

Patience and flexibility are the major attributes you will need as you assist these folks. But you'll learn a lot and build good friendships with some fine people. If you actually do the purchasing for the elderly people, ask them to be as specific as possible about what they want, and be sure to be as frugal as you can be in fulfilling those desires.

This is a good Saturday morning activity for multiple members of your group. Meet for breakfast, pray together, and then head out to shop—or do the shopping first and meet up for lunch with the other members of your group.

DEAR GOD, Thank you for the ability to run to the grocery store and take care of other errands at our convenience. Sometimes we take those opportunities for granted. Please open our eyes to places where we can serve. Give the people we're serving energy and strength. Use our relationships to teach each other more about you. IN JESUS' NAME, AMEN.

Reflect

- Did this experience change the way you view the convenience of being able to run to the grocery store whenever you want? If so, how?
- What questions can you ask during your time together that can teach you more about this person's life?

Helpful Hints

- This is a great opportunity to reach out to those in your community who are *not* involved with your church. Look around the neighborhood. If you see people who might need help, take time to get to know them and offer to help.
- After delivering the groceries, help unpack and put them away.
- Once in a while, buy fresh flowers on your own dime as a fun surprise!
- If there is a local grocery service via phone or Internet, you could also offer to help set up a regular delivery or at least to explain how it works.

Back-to-School Kits

"For wisdom will enter your heart, and knowledge will fill you with joy" (Proverbs 2:10).

Serving underprivileged kids.

One of the rites of passage for adults is that first stirring of nostalgia, especially about elementary school days. Even if they didn't like school, few didn't enjoy the annual rush of buying all new school supplies and feeling ready to go. Your group can provide that feeling for children who might not otherwise ever experience it.

Most school districts hand out lists of what children of each grade should have when they go back to school. Your group can get one of those lists and pool resources to purchase the needed items. It's OK to be a little extravagant if your group wants to provide kids with items *they* always desired but never owned in their own school days.

Pack all the purchases in an age-appropriate book bag, label it with the grade level of the contents, and pass it on to an agency that distributes supplies.

DEAR GOD OF WISDOM, *Thank you for providing a place to learn—a place where students can learn to serve you well in the ways that you made them. God, please protect students as they begin the school year. Keep them from injury and sickness. Thank you for people who have a passion to teach. Please use them to encourage and educate each student in his or her specific ways. IN JESUS' NAME, AMEN.*

Reflect

- How can you continue to provide and pray for children who go to the schools in your area?
- What are your favorite memories from the first day of elementary school? How has God used your experiences there to shape your life?

Helpful Hints

- Make sure that the supplies are all allowed in the public schools in your area before purchasing them.
- If there's no way to indicate gender-specific items (for example: pink and flowery notebooks), keep them gender-neutral.
- If you're unsure what to purchase and are having a hard time finding a local supply list, ask a parent at your church for ideas.

Adult Day-Care Activities

Serving the elderly.

Families that care for elderly family members in their own homes often have to seek supplemental care during the day when the care-givers are at work. So adult day-care centers have flourished in recent years, catering to the needs of these families. Often these centers care for widely divergent groups of elderly and disabled adults, providing health care and offering activities for their clients. But often they are understaffed and can't possibly provide the level of personal contact that many people desire.

Your small group could choose a particular time each week or month to visit with and provide activities for the clients at a local adult day-care facility. After discussing options with the professional staff, your group could create a rotating schedule of entertaining activities. Talent shows, bingo and other games, and singalongs are all popular options. This is one setting where the staff will allow or might even encourage Christian music and teaching.

"Stand up in the presence of the elderly, and show respect for the aged. Fear your God. I am the Lord" (Leviticus 19:32).

DEAR GOD, Thank you for opening our eyes to a community from which we can learn so much. Forgive us for all the times we've ignored our elders. Open our minds to ways we can learn from people who have so much wisdom.

Comfort these people as they struggle with physical problems. Take away any pain, and relieve those who are suffering. IN JESUS' NAME, AMEN.

Reflect

- What was most memorable about this experience?
- What did you learn about yourself and the residents?
- How can you continue to learn from people who have decades of wisdom to share?

Helpful Hints

- Ask around your group to see if someone has an elderly person living with his or her family, and that way, you can connect on a more personal level with a care facility and at least one family.
- Before your first visit, brainstorm questions that you could ask. Take advantage of this opportunity to learn from decades of life experience.
- Take time to build relationships with the employees of the facility, as well. This can be a great ministry to those who serve through their occupations in this way on a regular basis. They can also be a fantastic resource for learning about the specific needs of the elderly people.

70

"Will Work for Food" Pantry

"Then Jesus took the loaves, gave thanks to God, and distributed them to the people. Afterward he did the same with the fish. And they all ate as much as they wanted" (John 6:11).

Serving the hungry.

Sometimes we can be caught between two competing impulses—giving to those who ask, yet being suspicious about people who make their needs known. This is especially true with individuals who stand by the side of the road with "will work for food" signs.

One solution is a "will work for food" pantry at an accessible location where group members can store up single-serving-size foods. Group members can load up bags of nutrition and take them out to "the street."

To provide for someone on the side of the road, the food can't require a can opener, cooking, or utensils. Single-serving tuna fish snack kits, energy bars, pop-top pudding packs that don't require refrigeration, peanut butter crackers, bottled water, and granola bars are all ideal foods for such a pantry.

DEAR JESUS, At times, it's hard to understand so much brokenness and so much need in the world. Please give us hearts that break like yours. Take away any numbness, and show us how to have compassion as you would. Please give us the courage and wisdom to pray for and provide for the needs of others. IN YOUR NAME, AMEN.

Helpful Hints

- Choose foods that are high in protein—they're filling and healthy, especially for people who may not be getting the best nutrition on a regular basis.
- Go out in pairs. Especially for women, this is a safer option.
- Take a few minutes to sit down and talk with the people you're feeding.
- Offer but don't force prayer after your conversation.
- If you have a shelter, food pantry, or other services available at your church, bring information about those options. Don't be afraid to invite people you meet to church, as well.

Reflect

- Describe your comfort level during this project.
- Who and what surprised you while you served?
- How did this experience change your perspective on homelessness?

Hospital Hobbies

Serving the sick.

If you've ever had an extended stay at a hospital, or know anyone who has, you understand how the days can get long and boring away from home. Help to lift spirits by collecting materials to make fun activity kits for hospitalized patients at your local medical center.

"Hope deferred makes the heart sick, but a dream fulfilled is a tree of life" (Proverbs 13:12).

Begin by contacting your local hospital volunteer association to find out where and when you can deliver your donations. Three to four weeks before your planned delivery date, your small group should advertise to your church community that you're holding a drive to collect supplies for the activity packs. You may want to ask for donations that focus on specific care units (cancer patients, cardiac patients, and the children's wing) so people can tailor their donations to a specific audience.

Some objects that you may want to suggest for inclusion are general-interest magazines (such as Time or People), magnetic travel games, decks of cards, clean-joke books, word- or number-puzzle books, coloring books and art supplies, stationery and stamps, plastic putty, and small jigsaw puzzles.

One week before your planned delivery, take stock of the items you have received, and go shopping for other items needed to fill out the kits. Finally, hold a fun group get-together to assemble the activity packs, and afterward go bless the hospital patients by delivering your donations!

DEAR GOD, Please help these hospital patients to realize that there are people in this community who love them and are thinking about them during their hard times. Help our activity packs to brighten their days and bring them and their families the hope and faith they need to get through their trials. IN JESUS' NAME, AMEN.

Reflect

- What were some of the emotions and reactions of the patients when they received their activity packs?
- Which patient made the biggest impact on you, and why?
- In what ways do you hope to leave a long-term impact or impression with the patients, their families, or the hospital staff through this service activity?

Helpful Hints

- If you are creating activity packs for children, ask for the help of your own kids in shopping or donating items that others their age would enjoy.
- Try creating some packs that include foreign-language materials for those who aren't fluent in English.

72

Pamper a Precious Pooch

"The godly care for their animals" (Proverbs 12:10a).

Serving guide dogs.

We've all seen them...calm, steady, focused, regal...panting as they stroll along the sidewalk. Guide dogs are amazing animals that work hard for their owners day in and day out. But sometimes the limitations of their owners prevent these gentle leaders from getting the care they need. This project will set you in motion to provide grooming for a service dog.

Contact your local guide dog training organization to find out how you can connect with those willing to receive your services. Begin by calling your local 4-H chapter or searching for "guide dogs" in an Internet search engine. Set up an appointment to have two group members visit the home of the service animal.

Collect necessary dog-grooming supplies, checking with the dog's family before you go to see if there are any special concerns of the animal that need to be met. Supplies you should gather include a large wash bin, doggy shampoo and conditioner, canine-specific toothpaste and toothbrush, dog nail trimmers, brushes or combs, towels, and plastic gloves and cover-ups for the volunteers!

During the grooming, let the owner supervise (this will also help the dog to feel comfortable). When it's time to leave, you can offer to leave the supplies behind for future use. Be sure to "thank" the animal and the human for letting you come pamper this special companion.

DEAR GOD, Thank you for creating animals with unique skills that can help us through life. Through our act of service, help these guide dog owners to realize that God cares for them and their animal companions. Please bless all of the members of these special families. IN JESUS' NAME, AMEN.

Helpful Hints

- Wear comfortable, quick-drying clothing. You may also want to cover up with ponchos or plastic aprons to help keep dry.
- Bring a small stash of dog treats to reward the animal for a job well done, or to help reassure him during the grooming process. Check with the owner first to find out what the animal's favorite treats are.
- Talk with the owner(s) of the dog, and work to establish a relationship.

Reflect

- What were some interesting conversations you had with the owners? What, if any, spiritual implications might those conversations have had?
- How did you feel God working through this experience?

Using Language

Serving those who can't speak English.
Communication can be tricky enough when two individuals speak the same language, but imagine how tough it would be to know very little English. Buying groceries, pumping gas, and renting a movie become difficult daily activities when one doesn't comprehend the dominant language.

"If I could speak all the languages of earth and of angels, but didn't love others, I would only be a noisy gong or a clanging cymbal" (1 Corinthians 13:1).

Chances are someone in your small group has at least a basic knowledge of a second language that is common in your community. Use this information to put together a sheet of day-to-day English phrases with their appropriate translations, much like what you might use when traveling through a foreign country. Distribute this sheet within your small group, and use it the next time you find yourself in line behind someone who doesn't speak English. Attempt a phrase or two, and you'll be blown away by the response. Communicating with people in their own language means more than you can imagine.

Dear Creator God, You have created peoples of different places, cultures, races, and beliefs. It's our goal to connect with people in a meaningful way using their own language. Please speak through our words and communicate our love. Thank you for the variety and beauty of life. In Jesus' name, amen.

Reflect

- What did it feel like to help a person in his or her own language?
- How did people respond when you greeted them in their native tongue?
- What has this activity shown you about the importance of language?

Helpful Hints

- Saying "Hello" in Arabic or "Have a nice day" in French will communicate much more if you say it with a smile.
- When you put together a translation list, think about languages that are common in your community. This will aid in the process of actually using them.

All God's Creatures— Great and Small!

"Then God said, 'Let us make human beings in our image, to be like ourselves. They will reign over the fish in the sea, the birds in the sky, the livestock, all the wild animals on the earth, and the small animals that scurry along the ground' " (Genesis 1:26).

Serving animals in shelters.

Usually when you hear the words *need* and *serve*, you automatically think of people. It's important to remember, though, that much of God's creation is not human yet still deserving of our best stewardship. Seek out a local humane society or animal shelter, and offer the services of your group for a Saturday. Make the effort to learn from these professionals about the needs of animals within your community. You'll be surprised at how the needs of animals go unnoticed, such as abuse, neglect, strays, and diseased populations. Make an impact in God's creation by giving back to the animals that are without homes and without love.

DEAR GOD, *You have created a varied and beautiful creation, full of creatures great and small. We thank you for the world we live in and ask that today we might be of service to part of your creation that goes unnoticed in our community. Break our hearts and teach us your love through serving these animals. IN JESUS' NAME, AMEN.*

Reflect

- What did God teach you about his creation today?
- Would you ever volunteer at an animal shelter again? Why or why not?
- What did you learn about the people who work at the shelter?
- What pieces of information will you take with you to apply to your own life?

Helpful Hints

- When you volunteer at the shelter, be ready! Wear work clothes, and show the people there that you have come to work.
- Apply what you have learned to your everyday life. Use compassion and mercy when you encounter animals.

Be Non-Hired Help

Serving single moms.

This activity will ease the responsibilities shouldered by a single mom, allowing her to spend fun time with her children.

Select a single mom who is stretched beyond her allotted 24 hours a day to give her the gift of a clean house. Contact her to offer to clean her house while she spends time with her children. Set a date that works with your group and with her. Politely ask her to pick up clutter before you come over so that you can clean to the best of your ability.

On cleaning day, bring rags, an extra vacuum cleaner, and any cleaning products you prefer using. Don't just vacuum and dust; scrub the floors, wipe down the doorknobs and doorframes, and wipe down the walls in young children's rooms. Make this the best cleaning her house or apartment has ever had!

DEAR GOD OF THE OPPRESSED, Thank you for your care and concern for all people, including single parents, widows, and children without one or two parents. May this family seek your comfort and love. Help us to show your passion to those in need. IN JESUS' NAME, AMEN.

Reflect

- How did the mom and her children respond to your gift?
- What did this teach you about God's love for his people?
- Did working at the single mom's home teach you more about the sort of struggles she has? How? How might this lead to more service in the future? What sorts of service could that include?

> "Pure and genuine religion in the sight of God the Father means caring for orphans and widows in their distress and refusing to let the world corrupt you" (James 1:27).

Helpful Hints

- If your group is large, consider having some people do yardwork, clean out gutters, or fix broken furniture and appliances. Try to get as many things done as possible!
- If the home is particularly messy, send over one person to help the single mom de-clutter. This is a big step, but it will help you be able to really clean and not have to work around piles of paper and clothes!

Growing Green Gardens

"The land produced vegetation—all sorts of seed-bearing plants, and trees with seed-bearing fruit. Their seeds produced plants and trees of the same kind. And God saw that it was good" (Genesis 1:12).

Serving the poor.

This project will benefit your poor neighbors by providing food as well as education on how to grow a garden.

Select a poor neighborhood in your city, preferably one where people have yards. Ask a family if they would be interested in planting a garden. If they are, begin work on this project in mid-spring (following whatever planting patterns are good for your region).

Compile your resources to buy garden supplies. Things to purchase include topsoil, seedlings, small gardening tools, a watering can, and gloves.

On the day you plant the garden, give one person from the family (preferably an older child who does not have a job) responsibility for the garden. Work with him or her to plant the seedlings. Write out care instructions as well.

Once the garden is planted, visit at least one time a week to assist with garden maintenance. Work with the child to take care of the garden; don't do it all yourselves! In the fall (or whenever the garden is producing a lot of vegetables), have a harvest celebration with the family, your small group, and perhaps the extended neighborhood. Eat a meal together, pray, and sing a song of thanksgiving to God for the fertile soil, seeds, and vegetables.

Dear Creator God, Thank you for your gift of soil and plants. May this garden encourage the family. May the responsibility of caretaking be something this child takes seriously and learns from. May we recognize the way you are growing us every day, just like these plants. In Jesus' name, amen.

Helpful Hints

- Do most of the poor in your area live in apartment housing? That's OK. Buy several large pots, and plant small plants in those.
- If the family is unfamiliar with how to prepare some of the vegetables, provide recipes or teach them how to prepare and enjoy the fruits of their labor.

Reflect

- How does working with the earth cause you to reflect on God's creation?
- How did the family respond to your gift of gardening?
- Did you see the child (or individual responsible for maintaining the garden) grow over the summer?

Making One Small World a Better Place

Serving those in group homes.

People don't often go to group homes because they want to. If it's the elderly, it's because they're sick or unable to care for themselves. If it's children, it's because their parents have neglected them or there are significant problems. The young and old alike rarely show up on the doorsteps of these facilities for pleasant reasons. However, these organizations do not exist to perpetuate negative situations. They are there primarily to bring hope into struggle and to provide a place to heal, recover, or rest.

"Suppose you see a brother or sister who has no food or clothing, and you say 'Good-bye and have a good day; stay warm and eat well'–but then you don't give that person any food or clothing. What good does that do? So you see, faith by itself isn't enough. Unless it produces good deeds, it is dead and useless" (James 2:15-17).

Your small group can make these places even more pleasant for the residents by fixing up or brightening the facilities.

Contact a local children's home, a retirement facility, or other type of resident center, and ask how you can help. They might have rooms that need painting or a garden that needs weeding—something that costs them money and time that might not be available. Volunteer for a day-long project, and if it's possible, bring all the necessary supplies.

DEAR GOD, Use our efforts to bless those in these homes. Thank you for these places that so unselfishly serve those who cannot help themselves, and teach us to follow their example. IN JESUS' NAME, AMEN.

Reflect

- What are the needs of the people who live at this facility?
- How are your needs similar, and how are they different?
- What was uncomfortable about the experience?
- How did you see God's love in this place?

Helpful Hints

- Offer your services, and be reasonable. Don't volunteer to work on the plumbing if you've never done it before; but if you're a small group of plumbers, go for it. But be sure to pick a project you can complete in the time you're there.
- Bring lunches, treats, and drinks so the staff doesn't feel like they have to provide food.
- Take time to get to know the organization, who they serve, and the people who volunteer or work there regularly.
- If it's appropriate, spend time with the residents.

Breakfast Special

"A third time he asked him, 'Simon son of John, do you love me?' Peter was hurt that Jesus asked the question a third time. He said, 'Lord, you know everything. You know that I love you.' Jesus said, 'Then feed my sheep'" (John 21:17).

Serving the hungry.

Shelters and food pantries all over the country provide shelter, clothing, and food to meet the needs of people who can't afford these basic privileges, but the clothes do not make themselves, the beds do not appear out of nowhere, and the food does not suddenly appear on the plates.

These organizations often rely heavily on volunteers to cut the vegetables, cook the eggs, and serve the meals. It's not a pretty job, and it's often thankless. Especially for inner-city shelters in tough neighborhoods, it can be a rough crowd, but Jesus didn't call people to only serve when it was pleasant, formal, and proper.

Volunteer with your small group to serve one meal a month. Pick a time that works consistently for everyone, and contact a local shelter, offering your services.

DEAR GOD, *It's hard to process why the world seems unfair at times. Please shine your light amidst the hopelessness and teach us how to serve the needs of others. Thank you for the way you have blessed us, and please help us share these blessings.* IN JESUS' NAME, AMEN.

Helpful Hints

- Breakfast is a great option. It means sacrificing a few hours of sleep, but it's a time that most people have available before heading off to jobs.
- Expect at least one person a month to have a conflict or be sick. Don't use that as an excuse not to show up, but if you're telling an organization that you'll have a certain number of people there, that many people will be scheduled to serve. Having fewer might mean that a task goes undone. Therefore, if you have five people in your small group, tell them that you'll have at least four present every time.

Reflect

- What makes you uncomfortable about putting yourself in this environment on a regular basis?
- Where do you see hope amidst so much hardship?
- What is one thing, or a few things, that you can commit to praying for over the next month until you serve again?

Senior Citizen Ball

Serving the elderly.

Bless those who have spent generations blessing others by throwing a senior ball. If your congregation has many seniors, you can host it

"For the despondent, every day brings trouble; for the happy heart, life is a continual feast" (Proverbs 15:15).

at your church to honor them. Or, to bless those outside your walls, host it at a local senior home.

Pick a location, date, and theme for the ball, and begin to advertise a month or two in advance to get people excited. Create posters to hang in your church or in the senior home where you're hosting it. Decide who the guests of the ball will be—will you invite solely seniors, or do you want to let family members know to come enjoy the ball with their loved ones?

You'll also need to decide if there will be a small ticket price, or if it can come out of the church's budget. You can keep costs down if you rely on volunteers rather than hiring help. Recruit volunteers to prepare drinks and hors d'oeuvres, to set up tables and a dance floor, to decorate, to serve the food, to DJ the event, to tear down tables and clean up after the event.

Think of creative ways to make the event a real blessing. Ask seniors before the event for their all-time favorite dance songs, and play them. Hand out a flower to each woman in attendance. Make sure you have volunteers at the ball to ask seniors to dance, to get them drinks, to talk to them, and to just generally ensure everyone has a great time.

DEAR GOD, We want to make each one of the people here tonight feel special and cared for. We pray that each of the seniors here tonight would experience your love and joy. Help us to be your ambassadors to them. IN JESUS' NAME, AMEN.

Reflect

- What did you learn from interacting with these seniors?
- Is it hard to reach out to those who seemingly can't give anything back?
- What does this teach you about God's love for *you?*

Helpful Hints

- Make sure the selection and volume of the music are appropriate for the demographics of your guests!
- This night is all about making these seniors feel honored and special. Make sure to be warm in greeting them, and get to know those who are alone.
- Hosting the ball at a home for seniors will guarantee that those who aren't mobile can still attend.

Happy Feet

"So he got up from the table, took off his robe, wrapped a towel around his waist, and poured water into a basin. Then he began to wash the disciples' feet, drying them with the towel he had around him" (John 13:4-5).

Serving the homeless.

Do you live in an urban area with many homeless people but are never sure just how you can help them? Here's a great way: Give their feet a break. Shoes that don't fit, socks with holes, untreated blisters, harsh weather, and much walking can all add up to some serious foot problems.

If your church is located in an area accessible to the homeless, host a foot clinic at your church. If not, team with a local shelter to hold a clinic. Your clinic can be simple or it can be big. Choose from the following ideas.

- Collect donations for high-quality socks in various sizes and for comfortable walking shoes in as many sizes as you can get your hands on. Fit each person at your clinic with a pair of good shoes and several pairs of socks.
- Have foot-soak stations where people can relax in a chair and give their tootsies a nice long rest in some steaming, hot water.
- Have a blister-care area with plastic bandages, antibacterial ointment, towels, and a washing area.
- Recruit registered nurses to volunteer to help treat blisters.
- Have literature or medical professionals available to advise on how to prevent and treat frostbite.

And for those with real Christlike hearts:

- Simply wash their feet. (It won't be pretty, but the disciples' feet weren't pretty either.)

Dear God, You love each one of these people intensely, and you long for them to know your love. Please help us be your hands as we serve these children of yours. Let this service be a felt blessing in their lives, and help us to have humble servant hearts. In Jesus' name, amen.

Helpful Hints

- If you can't find a location or want a simpler project, take shoes, socks, and plastic bandages to the street, and pass them out to those who need them.
- Hot cocoa or cider would be a nice touch while people's feet are soaking.

Reflect

- Was it difficult or scary to serve people in this way? Why?
- Were your stereotypes of homeless people challenged by this activity?
- What did you learn about Jesus' heart for others through this activity?

We-Care Packages

Serving the homeless.

Here's a service project to show those who are less-fortunate that someone cares about them!

Put together care packages for the homeless or people living in shelters. Let them know they aren't forgotten. Include practical things such as items necessary for hygiene: washcloths and towels or wet wipes, soap, tooth- and mouth-care items, and hairbrushes. Additional items that would be welcomed by people living on the street are candles, socks, hand lotion, and gloves. To ease daily living, you might put your items into a small backpack or cloth tote bag. Consider including a blanket, a hat, or sunglasses. If the care bags are for those in shelters that house children, include items appropriate for them, as well as a toy that might cheer them.

Work with local establishments to determine how best to distribute the care packages.

"Then these righteous ones will reply, 'Lord, when did we ever see you hungry and feed you? Or thirsty and give you something to drink? Or a stranger and show you hospitality? Or naked and give you clothing? When did we ever see you sick or in prison and visit you?' And the King will say, 'I tell you the truth, when you did it to one of the least of these my brothers and sisters, you were doing it to me!' " (Matthew 25:37-40).

DEAR LORD AND KING, *Show us how to care for others, and in so doing, care for you. Help us to love the perceived unlovable. Help us not to judge who deserves care, lest we be judged. As we put together our packages, give us creativity and wisdom in choosing what will be of most help to those in need.* IN JESUS' NAME, AMEN.

Reflect

- How do you usually respond to, or think about, people on the street?
- How did this project help you grow in your understanding of how we are called to serve those in need or care for the "unlovable" as Jesus did?
- What blessings did you receive as you worked to give others a blessing?

Helpful Hints

- Give a personal touch by including a significant verse, handwritten on an index card, with a short personal message of hope or care added.
- Gift certificates from fast-food restaurants can be a great surprise to add to your gift bag.
- Attend a meal at a mission, and ask those who serve or direct there, as well as individuals who use their services, what they would find useful to receive.

Give 'Em a Break

"Since God chose you to be the holy people he loves, you must clothe yourselves with tenderhearted mercy, kindness, humility, gentleness, and patience" (Colossians 3:12).

Serving families of those with special needs.

This service project can be a huge blessing to someone who has to keep going, day after day, while caring for someone with special needs.

Whether a family has a child with physical disabilities or an adult member with Alzheimer's disease, those who give constant care to a loved one could use a break from the ongoing—and sometimes grueling—task of providing care for him or her.

Choose a family or families with a special-needs family member, and provide the necessary care for the individual with disabilities to allow the family a chance to have a respite for a few hours, a day trip, or a weekend away.

After determining who will be the recipient of your service project, find out what is required in order to have members of your group provide care during the designated time. For example, if CPR certification is necessary, make arrangements to complete a class in time for your planned service.

Find out if you can help arrange the outing for the caregivers. Maybe supply transportation to and from a destination or arrange the activities or lodging. They may have in mind what they want and only need the time away. Or perhaps they don't even have ideas of where to go and the group can arrange all that is necessary to have an experience that will be refreshing and relaxing.

Dear loving Lord, Teach us to be clothed in tenderhearted mercy, kindness, humility, gentleness and patience. Show us how we can live out these traits for those in need. As we care for the needy so that others can rest, make us more like yourself so that we can serve others well and also serve you. In Jesus' name, amen.

Helpful Hints

- Arrange phone contact in case you need the usual caregivers. But also have resources available, such as other family members who know the care of the individual, so interruptions to those on break can be avoided if possible.
- Meet with the family beforehand to learn their routine and to develop ideas for how to best use the time spent with the special-needs individual.

Reflect

- How did your service project specifically benefit those who received the break?
- What did you learn about yourself from this project?
- What was most difficult for you?

Food, Glorious Food

Serving the hungry.

Use this service project to provide food to those in need.

> "John replied, 'If you have two shirts, give one to the poor. If you have food, share it with those who are hungry' " (Luke 3:11).

Put together food bags filled with canned, packaged, and boxed food items, and deliver them to families in need known to your church or community.

Set aside a month to collect nonperishable food items from the members of your church. Set up collection bins to hold the foodstuff as it comes in. Also, give volunteers empty grocery bags with lists of suggested items attached. Be sure to set a date by which the bags must be returned, filled with the items requested.

Once all the food is collected, divide it up for each of the chosen recipients. Sort the food so a good variety goes to each individual or family. Put the food into bags or boxes that are marked in a way to identify the recipient, with name, phone number, and address. Divide the deliveries among the members of the group. Each member will contact the recipient to plan a time for drop-off.

DEAR GENEROUS AND LOVING LORD, *We want to recognize where our provision comes from. We want to be generous. And we want to give to others because you have given so generously to us. Show us how. Help us during this service project to get the necessary food to the people who need it. Direct our ideas and the carrying out of those ideas.* IN JESUS' NAME, AMEN.

Reflect

- What challenges did you encounter in helping others in this way?
- How did the recipients respond to your efforts? Were there any surprises?
- What was the most satisfying experience of this project?

Helpful Hints

- Including grocery store gift certificates will allow recipients to also buy perishable items, such as produce and dairy products.
- Include a note with the bags to express your care to the recipients.
- Be sensitive to the recipients' feelings. It may be embarrassing for them to receive this kind of assistance. Be willing to adjust your plans according to their comfort level.
- You may also choose to include household items, such as tissue, paper towels, and laundry detergent.

Carpet Cleaning

"When God's people are in need, be ready to help them" (Romans 12:13a).

Serving the elderly and infirm.

It's a dirty job, but somebody has to do it. Or somebody *should* do it. But often, no one does because—well, it's a dirty job!

Cleaning carpets isn't fun, but the satisfaction of standing back and seeing a beautifully clean rug is well worth the effort. But some will never have that satisfaction because they physically can't do the work. The elderly and the infirm are two groups that come to mind.

Check with local churches, cancer societies, or civic groups to find people who, for whatever reason, aren't able to clean their own carpets. Maybe someone is recovering from surgery or lives alone and can't move the furniture as needed. Then step up and step in!

If you plan to make this an ongoing service outreach, you might want to purchase several carpet cleaners. The approximate size of vacuum cleaners, these noncommercial cleaners are relatively inexpensive and easy to handle. Or, if you're just planning a day or weekend of service, commercial cleaners are often for rent at grocery stores.

You'll want to travel in at least pairs so you'll have two people to move furniture, refill containers, and visit if time allows. This is a particularly helpful service project to do before the Thanksgiving and Christmas holidays, when just about everyone wants to spruce up their homes for guests.

Helpful Hints

- Check what the carpet is made of before cleaning. If it's an area rug, make sure to check the manufacturer's cleaning guidelines *before* you begin.
- Check the bottoms of the legs of all furniture pieces. Some legs have a circle of metal in the bottom of the leg that can leave a rust stain on a damp carpet. Place squares of waxed paper under furniture legs until the carpet is completely dry. (If you do this, offer to go back and remove the paper the next day.)

DEAR LORD, It's the little things that we can do that bring so much pleasure to others. Thanks for teaching us how to serve. IN JESUS' NAME, AMEN.

Reflect

- What was the best part of this service project? the worst part?
- What were you feeling before you started this project? Did your feelings change? How?
- What word would you use to describe how the recipient(s) of this project felt when you finished?

Tree Trimming

Serving the elderly and infirm.
Everyone loves to trim a tree at Christmas, right?

> "The Savior—yes, the Messiah, the Lord—has been born today in Bethlehem, the city of David!" (Luke 2:11).

Well, maybe not. Perhaps there's someone you know who is ill or recovering from surgery or cancer treatment. (Let's face it—it's a bit of work to haul out all of those boxes from the attic or basement and put them out of sight again!)

Perhaps there's a widow or widower who can't face the prospect of trimming the tree alone. Perhaps there's a family who just can't afford a tree.

You can help! First, determine your recipient and arrange a time for the tree-trimming party. Find out if the person has ornaments or if you need to provide them. He or she might already have an artificial tree. If not, ask what kind of tree he or she would like and how big it should be.

Try to allow several hours for your visit so you can provide the love and attention the holidays make us crave. Remember: This may be the only social call your recipient receives during the holiday season, so make it special! Bring Christmas music and decorated cookies. Sing carols. Ask the history of special ornaments as you place them on the tree.

And before you leave, tuck a wrapped gift under the tree. If you're serving a family with children, make sure to leave an age-appropriate gift for each child.

DEAR LORD, Thank you for the birth of your Son. Thank you for allowing us to help celebrate your love during this special season. IN JESUS' NAME, AMEN.

Reflect

- How did this project make your holiday more special?
- How would you describe the look on your recipient's face as he or she gazed at your finished tree?
- What other ways can you spread the joy of Jesus' birth?

Helpful Hints

- Before you buy a tree, check whether your recipient has allergies you need to be aware of. If an artificial tree is in order, you can often find quite nice ones at thrift stores during the holiday season.
- If the person lives alone, offer to come back and take down the tree.

Honoring Our Veterans

"Be strong and courageous" (Joshua 1:9a).

Serving veterans and their families.

Next Memorial Day or Veterans Day, follow the practice of Arlington National Cemetery and place a small American flag on the grave of every veteran in your local cemetery. It's a moving visual to honor those who have served our country.

Take time to read each headstone and think about the era that person served and what he or she might have endured on our country's behalf. After placing the flags, join together for a prayer honoring the veterans.

First, of course, obtain permission from the caretakers of the cemetery before placing your flags. Also, be sure to ask the cemetery's guidelines and timetable for removing the flags. If possible, see if you can get a mailing list of families whose veteran relatives are buried there, and invite them to your ceremony.

If you'd like to extend your veteran salute, visit your local veterans hospital. Take flags, snacks, and small gifts to the veterans there. Call ahead to see what would be most appreciated and the optimum time to visit.

DEAR LORD, Help us to be mindful of those who have served our country. Thank you for letting us live in a country so bountiful in blessings. IN JESUS' NAME, AMEN.

Reflect

- What was the most moving part of this project for you? Why?
- How else could you honor veterans throughout the year?
- What do you think is the hardest part of serving our country as part of the military? How could you help?

Helpful Hints

- Be sure to follow proper cemetery etiquette. Don't tramp over graves, don't be loud, and be respectful. Obtain a copy of your cemetery's rules, if available.
- For extra impact, see if someone in your small group plays the trumpet. Have the person play taps after your prayer ceremony.

Compassion Car Packs

Serving the hungry.

Shop for and assemble nonperishable compassion packs to carry in your cars. Include a juice or water bottle, an energy bar or vacuum-sealed chicken or tuna-salad pack, a cup of fruit, and a pudding snack along with a napkin and plastic utensils. You may also want to include personal hygiene items such as shampoo, toothpaste, and a toothbrush. Include a New Testament, along with information on how to have a relationship with Jesus. Covenant together to overcome whatever hesitancy you might have to reach out with compassion by giving these gifts to hungry or homeless people as you encounter them.

"Give generously to the poor, not grudgingly, for the Lord your God will bless you in everything you do. There will always be some in the land who are poor. That is why I am commanding you to share freely with the poor and with other Israelites in need" (Deuteronomy 15:10-11).

DEAR GOD, *Please protect the people we encounter. Give them safety and health. Most important, help them come to know you. Help them find shelter and a home. We pray for jobs and healing.*

We pray for eyes to see all *people as you see everyone. Please give us the wisdom and strength to use all the resources you've given us in ways that bring you glory. IN JESUS' NAME, AMEN.*

Reflect

- What surprised you in this experience?
- Describe one person you'll probably remember for a long time.
- How, if at all, did you find yourself uncomfortable and struggling in this experience?

Helpful Hints

- Keep one or a few of these packs in your car, under the seat, for easy access. This way, when you get to an intersection with someone standing there holding a sign and asking for donations, you can easily give them a package in the amount of time you'll be stopped at the red light.

- If you often pass by the same person or few people, make mini packs that have a variety of materials. Also include information on where someone can go for shelter and clothing. Make sure to add directions, hours of operation, and other guidelines that would be helpful.

- Don't just hand off the packs—take a few minutes to acknowledge each individual. Respect and normal conversation will likely mean more than any tangible item. Start as you would with anyone else and ask the person's name.

How Can We Help?

"I am writing to remind you, dear friends, that we should love one another. This is not a new commandment, but one we have had from the beginning. Love means doing what God has commanded us, and he has commanded us to love one another, just as you heard from the beginning" (2 John 1:5-6).

Serving abused women.

Contact a local safe house for abused women. Find out what services or supplies the women need. For example, maybe the safe house needs a vehicle, or maybe some of the women need help finding jobs. Some women may need money or household supplies such as pots, dishes, or vacuum cleaners. Perhaps your group could share vehicles to free up a vehicle to loan to the safe house one day a week. Perhaps someone in your group could provide help with writing résumés. Or perhaps your group could collect money or donate the items the safe house needs.

DEAR GENEROUS AND LOVING GOD, We pray for the women in these shelters. They've had hard lives, and we hurt for them. Please give us compassion and understanding as we engage with them. Help us to see how we can serve them best. IN JESUS' NAME, AMEN.

Helpful Hints

- If you are going to serve by helping with résumés, plan on spending a day or an afternoon at the shelter, and ask women to sign up for time slots ahead of time.
- If you are in a position to hire people yourself, consider offering jobs to women in need. You'll probably find some very skilled and hardworking women who would be incredibly blessed by someone giving them such an opportunity.
- Be careful to protect the anonymity of these women! Women escaping abusive relationships are often hiding from the abusers in their lives.
- If your church has a counseling service, see if they can donate a few hours each month to counseling women who are struggling to recover from severe emotional, physical, and spiritual issues.

Reflect

- How do you personally deal with such brokenness?
- What emotions do you associate with abusive situations?
- Where can you serve with your skills and passions in the future?

Making It Home

Serving immigrants.

Identify people in your area who are underprivileged and recent immigrants, such as migrant workers. Do all you can to learn about their needs and situations. Maybe they need safer or less-expensive housing. Or perhaps they need day care for their children or reliable transportation. Have your small group get involved in helping this group of people. Don't just donate money—get involved. Meet the people and form relationships. Find out how the system needs to change, and work for justice.

DEAR LORD, Thank you for providing for us! Please forgive us for the times we have kept our time and resources to ourselves. Please give the people we serve what they need and bless them in ways beyond their wildest imaginations! IN JESUS' NAME, AMEN.

Reflect

- Put yourself in their shoes—what sacrifices did this family make to be in the place where they are today, and what would you struggle with most?
- What are basic needs that this family has that you take for granted?
- When was a time that you felt underprivileged or on the outskirts of society? How can you use that experience to empathize with this family?

"Speak up for those who cannot speak for themselves; ensure justice for those being crushed. Yes, speak up for the poor and helpless, and see that they get justice" (Proverbs 31:8-9).

Helpful Hints

- To find kids clothes, either go to a thrift store, if you have a little money to spend, or ask families with children to see if they are ready to give away any clothing items. Explain how you've gotten to know a family who is in a tough situation, and see if they can help. Often, a family who is blessed financially could *easily* spare one or two pairs of jeans and a few shirts. They will not be missed at all, but it may be more than an underprivileged family ever fathomed.

- Talk to your lawyer friends! Immigration laws require being on top of every last detail and document. However, to those who don't speak English, this may be next to impossible. Try to find a lawyer who would be willing to simply look over forms and letters, and help the family follow through on the necessary legal steps.

- Ask at church and find someone who speaks the family's native language. See if that person would be willing to help teach conversational English. Knowing English will help with employment.

- Introduce the family to church. If there is a church in their neighborhood or community, connect them with a local pastor and congregation.

Six-Month Adoption

"So humble yourselves under the mighty power of God, and at the right time he will lift you up in honor. Give all your worries and cares to God, for he cares about you" (1 Peter 5:6-7).

Serving those who need a friend.

As a group, find a needy single mom, someone undergoing AIDS treatment, or someone else in your community who is in desperate need, and adopt the person for at least six months. If possible choose someone outside your church family. If no one in your group knows of such a person, contact your church or your local social service organization.

Care for the person and offer love to him or her. Be a friend, offering financial help, transportation, food, companionship, or whatever else is needed. Ask the person to join your group. If you feel led, invite him or her to go to church with you, but remember: Your goal is not to get the person to church; your goal is to serve him or her with no obligations and no strings attached. If you have an ulterior motive such as getting the person to church, your acts of service might be seen as self-serving or manipulative. However, if the person is not a Christian, be sensitive to God's leading, and share the gospel with him or her if it's appropriate.

DEAR JESUS, Thank you for loving this person, and for using us to show your care. Please humble us by this experience, and help us to see more of your love and who you are.

Helpful Hints

- Before smothering your adopted person with kindness, form a friendship (if one does not already exist). This will make it seem more natural.
- Be careful not to share that he or she is your new "project." That might be insulting and taken the wrong way.
- If you are having a hard time finding a person to serve, look around where you work. Think of all the "small ways" that you could help someone. Helping in "small ways" might not be a big deal to you, but it might mean the world to the person you are serving.

Bless this person through us and in other ways. Show your love and ultimately lead this person into to a relationship with you. IN YOUR NAME, AMEN.

Reflect

- What have you begun to notice about other people after being so intentional with one person?
- Describe your relationship with the person before and after the six months of intentional service.
- What questions did the person ask concerning your willingness to help?

Thank You!

Serving people who serve.

As a small group, pick a group of people who work in thankless jobs and are not often appreciated. Plan a celebration for them. For example,

> "Praise the Lord, for the Lord is good; celebrate his lovely name with music" (Psalm 135:3).

you might want to thank the paramedics who work in your area. You may want to thank the custodial staff or the nursery workers at your church or the teachers at a local high school or the staff at a homeless shelter.

For the celebration, consider sending a "party in a box." Choose a very large box. In the bottom, place party food such as a cake or cookies, chips, soda pop in tightly closed bottles, and paper goods. Put in a CD of fun party music. Next have each member of your group put in a card with an encouraging note. Fill the box to the top with inflated balloons, confetti and party streamers. Seal the box, put a note on the top explaining what's inside, and have everyone use markers to decorate the outside of the box. Deliver the box, and have a party.

DEAR GOD, Thank you for celebrations. Thank you for joy and for laughter. Thank you for friendships, and thank you for those who serve in thankless jobs.

Bless the efforts of this group. Multiply their work in miraculous ways. Use them to share God's love by meeting the needs of others. Let them be refreshed and buoyed by our celebration. IN JESUS' NAME, AMEN.

Reflect

- How can you celebrate more of the little moments in life?
- What did you enjoy about this experience?
- When was a time someone celebrated you?

Helpful Hints

- Call ahead of time and find out when it would be ideal to give such a celebration—that way, the most people will be around and the food will be its freshest.
- Be careful to pick more generic food and treats (or a variety of specialty foods) so the most people possible will enjoy them.

Scheduled Giving

"For the world offers only a craving for physical pleasure, a craving for everything we see, and pride in our achievements and possessions. These are not from the Father, but are from this world. And this world is fading away, along with everything that people crave. But anyone who does what pleases God will live forever" (1 John 2:16-17).

Serving the needy.

Have everyone in your group agree to follow this schedule of giving:

Day One: Find one item in your home, and give it to someone who could better use it. Make sure you give away a useful, unbroken item. Do not replace any items you give away.

Day Two: Find two items in your home, and give them away.

Day Three: Find three items, and give them away.

Day Four: Find four items, and give them away.

Day Five: Find five items, and give them away.

Day Six: Find six items, and give them away.

Day Seven: Find seven items, and give them away.

By the end of the week, you'll have given away 28 items. A couple who does this activity separately will have given away 56 items. A group of 10 people doing this activity will collectively give away 280 items!

DEAR GOD, We are amazed at the ways you have blessed us with so many material possessions! Thank you! But God, sometimes we are selfish with these things. We put more value on them than you want us to, and we forget to pass on the blessing to others. Please help us use the resources you've given us to bless others. We ask that you open our eyes to the specific things that we don't need but would be helpful to others. IN JESUS' NAME, AMEN.

Helpful Hints

- Pick a theme for each day, such as clothes, kitchen stuff, or desk things.
- If there's anything you haven't used or worn in over a year, it's a safe bet that you won't miss it and someone else would appreciate it even more.
- Take a risk and give away something you really like. Make a sacrifice, and pray, asking God to help you understand more about what it means to truly give up something for others.

Reflect

- Did giving get harder or easier through the week?
- How do you feel now about how much stuff you have?
- Is this a discipline you could incorporate into your life regularly?

Caring About Foster Care

Serving those in foster care.

Get involved in your county's foster-care system. Learn as much as you can about the children typically served in your area. Call your county's child services department, and find out how you can help. Some areas welcome having small stuffed animals, blankets, picture books, toiletries, formula, or diapers to be used by children when they come under the protection of the department. Gather supplies, and donate them to the department. Some in your group may be moved to sign up to be foster parents.

"Then he said to them, 'Anyone who welcomes a little child like this on my behalf welcomes me, and anyone who welcomes me also welcomes my Father who sent me. Whoever is the least among you is the greatest' " (Luke 9:48).

DEAR GOD, *Thank you for being the perfect Father. Thank you for loving us as your children. Thank you for caring for and protecting us.*

Please love and care for children in the foster-care system in special ways. Show them that even though their own families cannot take care of them that they are valued and loved in your *family. Bring them to homes that are oozing with your love and your truth. Teach them your ways.* IN YOUR SON'S NAME, AMEN.

Reflect

- What does it mean to you that you are God's child?
- How can you pray for children who are in the foster-care system—probably because of a difficult situation?
- How can you communicate God's love to a child who may have been rejected by his or her own parents?

Helpful Hints

- Take time to research and pray about accepting foster children. Plan a time to meet with those who have had experience.
- Tell parents of junior highers and high schoolers that you are looking for children's items. They may have closets and basements full of things that are too young for their teenagers!
- Plan for and take the time to wash and clean all the toys and clothes.
- Ask local businesses for donations to your cause. Oftentimes they will be excited to serve the community in this way.
- Before interacting with children, ask the local organization for a short briefing. Many children may have extremely painful and heartbreaking stories, not situations that you might be accustomed to dealing with.

Caring for At-Risk Youth

> "Now may our Lord Jesus Christ himself and God our Father, who loved us and by his grace gave us eternal comfort and a wonderful hope, comfort you and strengthen you in every good thing you do and say" (2 Thessalonians 2:16-17).

Serving youth in alternative high schools.

Volunteer to help in your community's alternative high school. Such schools often serve at-risk teenagers or teenagers who've been in trouble with the law or have substance-abuse problems. Some teenagers are responsible for providing a living for themselves. Others must juggle the responsibilities of school and children. Still others struggle to learn despite having learning disabilities. Perhaps the school in your community could use mentors. Perhaps your group could teach special skills in the school. Perhaps the group could take a turn caring for the students' children.

DEAR GOD, *Thank you for the education system. Thank you for the ability to learn.*

For whatever reason, these students were struggling and came to this school. Use it as a positive experience. Use it to teach them about who they are and to give them confidence in this. Give them skills and opportunities to overcome their current challenges.

We ask for discipline and patience for them. We ask for them to find hope when it is hopeless. Use us as a hope in their lives.

Show us where we can serve them and you best. Teach us to be patient, and use them to help us learn more about you. IN JESUS' NAME, AMEN.

Reflect

- What was challenging for you when you were in school?
- How were the students you worked with gifted? What were they passionate about? How can you encourage these gifts and passions?
- How did it feel to serve in this kind of situation?

Helpful Hints

- Some alternative high schools are interest-specific. If music is your passion, pick a music school. If you're a engineer, target a math and science school.
- Ask teachers for ideas and ways to help particularly difficult students.
- If you run a business and have the ability to do this, hire students at a school that specializes in job skills.

Children of the World

Serving orphaned children globally.
There are many countries in which orphaned
children have little hope for a good life. In
some countries, orphans live in garbage dumps

> "Help him to defend the poor, to rescue
> the children of the needy, and to crush
> their oppressors" (Psalm 72:4).

and make their living by going through the garbage. In other countries,
disabled children are forgotten in sterile hospitals with substandard care
and no one to show them love. Find out what your church or denomina-
tion is doing to help orphans in other countries, and see how your group
can get involved. Another way to help is to get involved with organizations such as World Vision and Compassion International.

_DEAR LORD, Please shine your love with extreme intensity on those who are
without parents. Show them that you love and value them. Bring into their lives
adults to teach them about you and who love them only second to loving you.
Bless them with families—even though they may not be biologically related.
Heal those who are in pain and suffering from disabilities and disease. Bring
caring people to their side to hold them and care for them. Bring doctors with
medicine._

_Lord, it is humbling to think that they have
so little while we have so much. Help us be
more aware of these situations and to do something about it more often. Thank you for the
ability to serve these children. Thank you for
calling us your children. IN JESUS' NAME, AMEN._

Reflect

• How has God been a Father to you?
• How have your parents shaped you?
• When have you felt orphaned, and how
has God comforted you?

Helpful Hints

• You could even plan a trip to visit and
serve at an orphanage.
• Be careful what you send to a foreign
country! In many countries, particularly
developing ones, there is a fee for
picking up packages at the post office.
Sadly, packages are searched, and items
of value are stolen. Check with local
missionaries or organizations to ask about
how to ensure that your efforts reach the
children.
• If a group or a person is going overseas
for a short-term missions trip, see if you
could pack an extra suitcase of toys and
supplies for them to take to the children.
This will bypass the postal system and
give the person or group of people another
connection to a local ministry.

Showing Mercy

"Share your food with the hungry, and give shelter to the homeless. Give clothes to those who need them, and do not hide from relatives who need your help" (Isaiah 58:7).

Serving the weak.

Merciful people often take up the cause for those who are too weak or powerless to protect themselves. Investigate in your area and find a group of people who need help. Perhaps there are many homeless people in your area. Or perhaps there are many children with parents in prison. Or perhaps there are many elderly in your area who are separated from their families. Discuss what your group can do financially, socially, and politically to show mercy to that group. Then carry out your plans.

DEAR GOD, Thank you for showing us ways to serve. Thank you for giving us the opportunity to serve others. Please care for this group in amazing ways. Heal them in all ways. Show your power in their lives. God, please bring mercy to difficult situations. Provide for them in abundance! Teach us through this. Open our minds and hearts to receive love and blessing from those we are serving. IN JESUS' NAME, AMEN.

Helpful Hints

- Before offering services or interacting with a particular group, specifically when dealing with minors, make sure you are aware of any legal liability or concern.
- Because you might only serve for a short time, it might be more effective to partner with a local organization who provides long-term service and care. This way, you can work alongside what they already have going, and when your commitment time is up, you will not leave anything unfinished.
- Find out if your neighborhood has any programs to serve the weak and powerless, and see how you can make a difference in a very local way.

Reflect

- Why did you choose this particular group?
- How can you continue to pray for this specific group?
- How can you relate to this group?

Through God's Eyes

Serving those in prison and their families.

Are there ways your small group can get involved in prison ministry? Don't overlook your city or county jail, as well as providing services to families of those incarcerated (such as visiting, counseling, Bible studies). If it seems a bit scary to be

"So it is right that I should feel as I do about all of you, for you have a special place in my heart. You share with me the special favor of God, both in my imprisonment and in defending and confirming the truth of the Good News" (Philippians 1:7).

involved directly with prisoners, you can still be involved in a ministry. Organize your church's efforts to minister through Prison Fellowship's Angel Tree project. This ministry provides gifts for prisoners' children at Christmas. For more information, check out Prison Fellowship's Web site: www.pfm.org.

DEAR JESUS, Please humble us as we are about to reach out to a group that we're not that familiar with. Please help us see that we are just as sinful as these people, only our sin has not brought us to the same place. Therefore, please help us see these people with your eyes—as people you created and love. Open up their hearts to a relationship with you. Use us in ways that are beyond what we could ever imagine. Thank you for this amazing opportunity! IN YOUR NAME, AMEN.

Reflect

- What was the most challenging part of this experience?
- How do you think God views prisoners? How can you see these people through his eyes?

Helpful Hints

- Partnering with your church or an organization will help with safety and logistical issues.
- If you are reaching out to people who are no longer in prison or who are family members of prisoners, invite them to church.

A Special Service

"Children are a gift from the Lord; they are a reward from him" (Psalm 127:3).

Serving special-education teachers.

As a group, consider working with a special-education teacher. Special-education teachers can often use volunteer assistants in their classrooms. Special-needs kids often need more attention than one person can give. Your help in the classroom would be greatly appreciated—by the teacher and the kids. Be ready for anything, though—the teacher may need you to clean the classroom, spend time with an individual child, or simply walk among the children and help where needed.

Call the main office of your local school district to see who members of your group should contact.

DEAR GOD, Thank you for the education system. Thank you for children. Thank you for those children who have special needs. Use them to show your love. Remind them how special they are. Use their families to be an example in patience and love.

Thank you for bringing teachers into their lives. Give them (and us!) patience and wisdom in how to serve these children better.

Bring friends and laughter to the lives of these children. Help them feel comfortable with who they are. Heal their physical ailments. Show them how beautiful they are! IN JESUS' NAME, AMEN.

Reflect

- What, if anything, was challenging about this situation?
- Describe what kind of patience was required.
- How was this experience similar to or different from your other experiences teaching or working with children?
- Describe the learning process for these students and how it is like or unlike your own learning process.

Helpful Hints

- Talk to the school about any special training or orientation needed.
- Sunday school teachers could also use the assistance if they have children with special needs.
- Pick a time in your week that you can consistently volunteer, and make sure to stick to it. This will help the teacher when he or she is planning. Your group could also consider rotating weeks so each person goes in once a month.

Senior VBS

Serving the elderly.

Organize and conduct a vacation Bible school program in a nursing home! Those in the assisted living or nursing home often cannot come to the church, so go to them. Keep it simple. Some singing, a short Bible story, refreshments, a simple game, and closing songs are all things you could do.

"So let us celebrate the festival, not with the old bread of wickedness and evil, but with the new bread of sincerity and truth" (1 Corinthians 5:8).

DEAR GOD, Thank you for bringing generations together. Thank you for guiding our decisions and our enthusiasm for this project. Open our eyes to see the needs of the residents and our minds to learning from them. Thank you for the decades of wisdom and for the opportunity to spend time with them.

Please take away and forgive any judgment. Calm our fears and discomfort, and take away anything that prevents us from showing your love. IN JESUS' NAME, AMEN.

Reflect

- Describe one person you met whom you won't soon forget.
- How was this like or unlike other ways that you have served? What would you do differently if you were to do this again?
- A fast-paced society does not take time to sit and listen—to value or appreciate—those who are in the place in life that requires them to live in an assisted-living situation. When have you felt this way? How can you use that experience to show love to the elderly?

Helpful Hints

- Check with the residence home first to find out about any special needs, such as hearing aids, dietary restrictions, and vision issues. Make sure that your program works well for everyone!
- Find a nursing home where someone in your group has a personal connection. The already-established relationship will bring you credibility.
- Get to know the staff and serve them, as well! Offer to stick around during mealtime and do some of the serving work. Don't take their jobs away—just be available to offer a helping hand with things like carrying food trays to residents.
- Take your VBS on the road! Consider visiting several nursing homes over the course of a month.

Conversational Partners

"You must not mistreat or oppress for-eigners in any way" (Exodus 22:21a).

Serving international students.

Hundreds of thousands of foreign students study in the United States every year—many of them from countries closed to Christianity. They've come here to get a degree, but while they're here, they want to experience American culture. Often they're also interested in understanding what Christianity is all about. Unfortunately, most of them will make few American friends, and only a tiny percentage will ever see the inside of an American home.

Nearly every college and university with any enrollment of international students has some sort of "conversational English" program for their students from non-English-speaking countries. Call your local college's international student services office, and offer your services. They will caution you about proselytizing students, which you can assure them you're not about. You're here to befriend and to serve.

Most international students have a fairly good grasp of English, as they usually have to pass language proficiency tests to enroll in schools here. However, they're often insecure about their English and deeply desire to talk more like Americans. Conversational partners get together at an agreed-upon time just to talk. The Americans gently help with pronunciation and vocabulary, but the basic format is simply to talk about your respective lives and countries.

DEAR GOD, Thank you for creating a world so diverse and beautiful! Thank you for merging these worlds through the college experience. Open our eyes for new ways to reach out to these students. Besides a little more about a language and a culture, teach these students about you. IN JESUS' NAME, AMEN.

Helpful Hints

- If you have the space and resources, consider hosting an international student.
- Ask questions and learn from these students! They are probably curious about life in the United States, but they also have a lot to offer!
- If several members of your group do this, celebrate the end of each semester by bringing all the conversational partners together for a party.

Reflect

- What did you learn about the students and their countries?
- How do you think God views the church internationally?
- What does faith look like in the students' homelands?

Tutoring Kids

Serving at-risk kids.

Large numbers of children in America grow up with little support or encouragement from adults. Tragic at all ages, especially in middle and high school, the lack of role models and mentors has many educational, social, and spiritual consequences.

Communicate with the guidance counselor of a middle school or high school near your church. Offer to provide free tutoring services, assuring the counselor that this isn't a smoke-screen for proselytizing. Let the counselor guide you on how to make your services available to the students. Recruit group members with an education in a variety of subjects, and set a time shortly after school is out for them to be available at your church facility.

You'll spend time helping kids with math and history, but you'll also hear heartbreaking stories about family situations and precarious circumstances. Your numbers will fluctuate wildly, and some students you come to care about may just stop coming. But keep in mind that you are planting seeds of truth and watering lives with love.

DEAR JESUS, Thank you for teaching us about you. Thank you for the education you provided and the ways that we can use that to teach others. Bless these students each and every day at school. Shine your love through us. IN YOUR NAME, AMEN.

> "In the same way, encourage the young men to live wisely. And you yourself must be an example to them by doing good works of every kind. Let everything you do reflect the integrity and seriousness of your teaching. Teach the truth so that your teaching can't be criticized. Then those who oppose us will be ashamed and have nothing bad to say about us" (Titus 2:6-8).

Reflect

- What were some things that you struggled with when you were the age of these students you're working with?
- Describe the person you connected with the best.
- What are some other ways you can serve and pray for these students?

Helpful Hints

- You might also contact your church's youth ministry to connect with students who need a little extra help.
- Get to know the parents, as well! They'll love knowing more about the people spending time with their children.
- If your building has a family life center, gym, or other less-threatening area, use that for the tutoring center. Have light, inexpensive, and healthy snacks available. Don't overwhelm those who venture in with too much attention.

Scripture Index

Duration Index

Serving Your Community

One-Time Ideas 10, 14, 17, 18, 20, 21, 22, 23, 26, 28, 29, 30, 32, 33, 35

Short-Term Projects 15, 16, 19, 24, 27, 31

Ongoing Services 11, 12, 25, 34

Serving Your Church

One-Time Ideas 38, 40, 41, 46

Short-Term Projects 39, 43, 44

Ongoing Services 42, 45, 47

Serving Your Small Group

One-Time Ideas 50, 54, 55, 56, 58

Short-Term Projects 52, 53, 57

Ongoing Services 51, 59

Serving Your Friends and Family

One-Time Ideas 63, 64, 70, 71, 72, 75, 76, 77, 78, 81

Short-Term Projects 62, 65, 67, 69, 79

Ongoing Services 66, 68, 73, 74, 80

Serving Those With Specific Needs

One-Time Ideas 84, 89, 90, 92, 93, 95, 97, 98, 100, 103, 104, 109, 117

Short-Term Projects 86, 94, 99, 101, 102, 106, 107, 108, 110, 111, 113, 114, 115

Ongoing Services 85, 87, 88, 91, 96, 105, 112, 116, 118, 119

Types of Service Index

Seasonal Ideas Index

Checklist

	Date Used	Group Used With	Notes/Comments
Serving Your Community			
Light Up Your Neighborhood			
Work Recycling Program			
Neighborhood Share-a-Thon			
School Smart			
Run, Small Group, Run!			
Love Your Enemies			
Post-Game Pickup			
Nothing but Positive			
Adopt a Family Farm			
Recycling Day			
Facelift for an Eyesore			
Join In!			
Town Festival			
Furniture Fix-Up			
Cell Phone Recycling			
Serving the Servers			
One Man's Treasure...			
Help Carry the Burden			
A Bag Party			
A Gesture of Love			
Editorialize			
Prayer Walk			
Neighborhood Carwash			
Welcome to the Neighborhood!			
Ambush Lawn Service			
Serving Your Church			
Group Workday			
Sunday Morning Service			
Undercover Pastoral Care			
A Gift of Service			
An Opportunity to Serve			

	DATE USED	GROUP USED WITH	NOTES/COMMENTS
Bibliophiles			
Assistant to the Teacher			
A Talent to Serve			
Janitor's Day Off			
Orphans and Widows			

Serving Your Small Group

Service Scavenger Hunt			
The Great Child Exchange			
Pick a Name			
Honey-Do Wish List			
Day Cook-Off			
Cruising Around			
Mother's Day Dinner			
Party Packages			
Talent Teaching			
Birthday Buddies			

Serving Your Friends and Family

Small-Group Garden			
It's All in the Detail!			
Get the Gear Back in the Game			
Third Place			
Free Gym!			
Secret Service			
Encouragement Works			
Drive-Through Service			
Encouragement Post			
Power Progressive Housecleaning Party			
Shish Kebarbecue			
Free Help Yellow Pages			
Feeding on the Word			
Second Parents for a Day			
Picture Perfect			
Bake-Off			
Scripture Albums			
An Encouraging Week			
Serving Special Needs			
Carols and Cookies			

	DATE USED	GROUP USED WITH	NOTES/COMMENTS

Serving Those With Specific Needs

	DATE USED	GROUP USED WITH	NOTES/COMMENTS
A Night Out or a Makeover In			
Grocery Express			
Back-to-School Kits			
Adult Day-Care Activities			
"Will Work for Food" Pantry			
Hospital Hobbies			
Pamper a Precious Pooch			
Using Language			
All God's Creatures—Great and Small!			
Be Non-Hired Help			
Growing Green Gardens			
Making One Small World a Better Place			
Breakfast Special			
Senior Citizen Ball			
Happy Feet			
We-Care Packages			
Give 'Em a Break			
Food, Glorious Food			
Carpet Cleaning			
Tree Trimming			
Honoring Our Veterans			
Compassion Car Packs			
How Can We Help?			
Making It Home			
Six-Month Adoption			
Thank You!			
Scheduled Giving			
Caring About Foster Care			
Caring for At-Risk Youth			
Showing Mercy			
Through God's Eyes			
A Special Service			
Senior VBS			
Conversational Partners			
Tutoring Kids			